R Richardson-Gardner

A Trip to St. Petersburg

R Richardson-Gardner

A Trip to St. Petersburg

ISBN/EAN: 9783337144951

Printed in Europe, USA, Canada, Australia, Japan

Cover: Foto ©Andreas Hilbeck / pixelio.de

More available books at **www.hansebooks.com**

A TRIP

TO

ST. PETERSBURG.

In the hope of affording some little amusement to my friends, the following Letters have been reprinted from the " Windsor and Eton Herald," for private circulation.

R. RICHARDSON-GARDNER.

46, SUSSEX GARDENS, HYDE PARK,
    Christmas 1872.

Hôtel de Russie,

St. Petersburg,

16–28th *December*, 1871.

My dear John,

You kindly expressed a wish to hear how our party fared in undertaking such a long journey in the dead of winter; and so, in compliance with your request, I send you a few "jottings by the way," which I trust may interest you and our friends at home, although you must expect them to be very incoherent, and not be surprised to find that I run in my thoughts up and down the line, backwards or forwards, some odd thousand miles or so, to describe something, which occurred at some time, somewhere.

St. Petersburg sounds a long way off; and so it is; overland above two thousand miles, by Calais, Brussels, Cologne, Berlin, Kowno, Wilna, and Pskof; but our time has passed so pleasantly, in such agreeable society, with so much comfort and convenience, that on our arrival here, after five days' and five nights' journey, two nights of which were passed in beds and three in railway carriages, we found ourselves, after warm baths and a nice little supper, quite prepared to start again if necessary.

Well, our party consisted of Louise, myself, Colonel Money, (the accomplished writer of those interesting articles in *The Times* of September last, descriptive of the Russian autumn manœuvres), Lieut.-Colonel Isenbeck, (a distinguished officer in the Russian army, speaking English like an Englishman), Captain Chambers, (a Canadian officer on his way to the Caucasus), and a jolly party we were, the endeavour of each being to amuse and entertain the others, so as to wile away the hours which might otherwise have been felt to have been long and wearisome.

To begin at the beginning, as the story books say, we first of all paid a visit to Nicholay's, the extensive furrier, in Oxford Street, for our Russian outfit, which comprised a regular suit of furs, clothing ourselves *cap-à-pie*, from head to foot, in the skins of wild beasts; with this advantage over the inferior animals, that we wear their fur next our bodies, by turning them inside out, or outside in, which is it? as Dundreary would say. My "shuba," (a long fur cloak), cap, boots, and gloves are of beaver; Louise patronised the lynx, Colonel Money was enveloped in racoon, Colonel Isenbeck in bear, and Louise turned out her maid (Bateson) as a kangaroo. I must consult Darwin, and ascertain whether there is any natural affinity in his theory, between either of us and the animals whose skins we inhabit, or whether, in the event of our wearing them long enough, we are likely to return to our aboriginal or abnormal state. We should make the fortune of Wombwell's menagerie, if we offered ourselves for exhibition on our return.

Among other desirable things we provided ourselves with, were a pic-nic basket, fitted up with four knives and forks, plates, tumblers, d'oyleys, two wine bottles with screw corks, a butter bowl, tin for preserved meats, salt, pepper, mustard boxes, &c., which we had carefully filled at Fortnum and Mason's with collard tongue, Yorkshire pies, *pâté de foie gras*, Bolognas, and solid beef tea, so as to be prepared for a campaign on the road, in the event of our being snowed up, which does occasionally happen, besides being useful whenever the qualms of hunger overtook us, and no refreshment-room within reach. Then we laid in an "Etna," and spirits of wine, railway reading lamps on an improved principle, purchased at Argand's, in Bruton Street, a chess board, with men moving on pegs fitted into holes in the board, india-rubber things to be inflated so as to support the back, very much in the form of (pray don't mention it) a lady's bustle, a thermometer and barometer in Morocco cases, and Murray's hand books for North Germany, Russia, Poland, and Finland, &c. &c.

Wishing our friends good-bye, and being all prepared with first-class through tickets to St. Petersburg, with 28 coupons for places *en route*, off we started by 8.45 p.m. train from Charing Cross for Dover and Calais, leaving the latter place for our 2,000 miles journey in the early hours of the morning, with a carriage to ourselves, and Colonel Money, and the other gentlemen with one to themselves, all tucked up and made ready for a comfortable nap, in which we all thoroughly indulged; and, as at this moment writing to you from my hotel at St. Petersburg, I find it is time to retire, I will say good night, and resume my "jottings by the way" to-morrow morning.

A fine fresh morning, clear and frosty, with the sleighs dashing about, and everyone looking happy and cheerful. Thermometer a few degrees below freezing point outside, with a delightful atmosphere in our rooms of about 65 degrees Fahrenheit, kept at that temperature all day and all night through. But I forget that my jottings have not yet brought me *here*, so I must not anticipate. Let me see; where was I last night? Leaving Calais, fast asleep, to wake up at Lille, where *café au lait* was the order of the day. By-the-bye, who has ever been offered one franc paper notes in France before the late calamitous war? I have made this same early repast at Lille a dozen times on my visits to the continent, but silver coinage was always in abundance; but now, alas! those barbarous Germans have despoiled poor France of all its silver and gold, and she has been obliged to retrograde to a small paper currency, while the victorious Prussians have reconverted their paper thalers into delightful little gold pieces of 5, 10, and 15 thalers each.

First night passed in railway carriages; second night in bed at Cologne, and glad we were to get out of the place next morning, famed as it is for its typhoid disagreeables, which no number of their Jean Marie Farinas, with any quantity of their famous *eau*, is capable of dispelling from the olfactories. The cathedral tower, however, I am glad to inform you, has much progressed since your last visit. The King of Prussia, I hear, pays towards its completion a million thalers a year, which, poor fellow, he can well afford now, if Bismarck lets him in for a share of the French spoil. Now, for Berlin, passing on the way Krupp's cast steel factory, famed for the production of colossal ordnance of the most scientific kinds. The enormous scale of his works is shown by the fact that they cover 450 acres of ground, and employ 8,000 men and 195 steam engines. Let Manchester and Birmingham look to their laurels, or rather to their pockets; but I can give them one scrap of comfort, that on trial, Krupp's have been surpassed by Armstrong's, and I read in the paper that an enormous steel gun of Krupp's burst the other day at Cronstadt, and killed a few people, but, unfortunately for Armstrong, Krupp wasn't there.

Through the pass called Porta Westphaliæ. In the neighbourhood of this pass is supposed to have occurred the great battle in which the German general Arminius defeated the Roman army under Varus with terrific slaughter. It is well known that this defeat put a stop to the advance of the Romans into northern Germany; Varus killed himself after the battle, but his head was sent to the Emperor Augustus, at Rome, who was so dejected by the news, that for several days he scarcely spoke except to say, " *Vare, Vare, ubi sunt legiones meæ.*"

On, on, through Hanover and Brunswick, with a sympathetic feeling, as we pass, for the poor blind king and his troubles, and the warlike race of Brunswick, nine of whose princes are interred in the vaults of the cathedral of St. Blaize, all of them having perished in the field of battle; among them are the bodies of the duke who was mortally wounded at the fatal battle of Jena, and of his son, who fell at Quatre Bras, having nobly avenged his father's death at the head of his devoted black band. First view of the Elbe at Magdeburg, frozen into blocks of ice. There Luther went to School, as a poor chorister, often sung at rich men's doors to earn a scanty pittance, and here the ferocious Tilly, after carrying the citadel by assault, after two year's siege, massacred 30,000 of its inhabitants, without regard to age or sex, and burnt the church of St. John, where many hundred women and children had taken refuge. Is it not Milton who our father used to quote, as saying that " Man's inhumanity to man makes countless thousands mourn " ?

Through Potsdam, the Prussian Versailles, (when we had a view of some of its magnificence, but which we shall visit more particularly on our homeward journey) into Berlin, about eleven o'clock at night, where carriages awaited us (by telegraph) to convey us to the Hôtel du Nord, Unter den Linden. Now, my dear John, I don't know what your idea is of Berlin, but my first impressions are those of disappointment as regards the town in its external aspect, but I may be more pleased on our return, when we shall have time to visit its art treasures, &c. The great Brandenburg gate, an imitation of the Propylæum at Athens, is grand; but when I remember the magnificent triumphal arch at Milan, the comparison is not in favour of Berlin. They both exhibit cars of victory on their summit, but the Milanese is by far the superior work of art. The statue of Frederick the Great, the colonnade of the Museum, the Arsenal, and one or two other public buildings, comprise the principal architectural and artistic beauties; but I must not forget to mention the beautiful statues by Kiss, the Amazon which we had at our great exhibition, and another of St. George and the Dragon, which I had never seen before, and shall never forget. I went to gaze at it three times in twenty-four hours; but I don't intend to weary you with descriptions, all of which may be found in Murray, but rather to jot down little things as they occur on our route. Let me advise you, if you come abroad, not to go to Prussia for some little time, as although we have personally experienced no discourtesy, I feel sure there is a latent unfriendly feeling towards the English by the Prussians since the late war, an opinion which has been confirmed by several with whom I have lately spoken on the subject. In fact, I witnessed it on more than one occasion, notably at the railway station, when we were leaving for Russia. There happened to be some dispute between a Prussian Droshki driver and an Englishman, and soon a crowd gathered round and became very insolent and even menacing to the Englishman, who in this case was clearly in the right, but who had Prussian hands laid upon him, which I fully expected would have ended in a fight. If such had happened, our party of four men were quite prepared to take his part and save him from maltreatment, however unpleasant or undignified it might have been to be hustled by a lot of Prussian roughs. The upper classes do not, of course, show it in this fashion, *but it exists, whatever be the cause of it*, and the lower orders manifest physically that which the superior orders incline to mentally. The Imperial Palace, or "Schloss," built by the father of Frederick the Great, is a fine old palace, used chiefly now for Court ceremonials, the King inhabiting a smaller, but probably more comfortable place of residence; but I was really surprised that his majesty should allow the exterior of his ancestral palace to remain in such a disreputable state. It is in a disgraceful state of *want of repair*. Again I hope that some of the Frenchman's "shekels of gold and of silver" may be applied to the re-adornment of his Majesty's heritage.

Next night, eleven o'clock p.m.—Take our place from Berlin to St. Petersburg—two nights' and two days' travel. Let us look about us and see what our arrangements are. Louise and I have a double compartment-carriage, each opening out into the other by a door between; the one making up into beds for the night and the other forming our compartment for the day, all heated most genially by hot water pipes laid on from the engine boiler. Good. Our commissionaire who we sent to engage this extra comfort for us carried out his instructions well. What have Colonel Money and our other companions got? After settling ourselves we issue forth to find them out; nothing could be better. A large saloon carriage, heated by a wood-burning stove, and all of them seated round smoking their cigars, with another companion who I have not mentioned before, but whom I will introduce to you now. A tremendous, large, handsome mastiff dog, bought by Colonel Isenbeck of the famous Bill George, of Canine Hall, Kensal New Town, lay stretching himself at full length in the middle of the saloon, and what do you think they had christened him, painting his name in large letters on his temporary leather collar, ROGER! Was it not too bad of the Russian colonel? Some of the fellows had put him up to it, to have a joke with me; however I patted him on his back and said he was called after a very good fellow, although a political opponent, and Roger has fared sumptuously every day, and formed one of our party, travelling in first-class carriages right through to St. Petersburg. And, now, returning to our carriage and settling ourselves for the night, I will reserve the remainder of our journey until my next letter.

I remain, your affectionate Brother,

R. RICHARDSON-GARDNER.

JOHN C. RICHARDSON, ESQ.
   Glanbrydan Park, Carmarthenshire.

HÔTEL DE RUSSIE,

ST. PETERSBURG,

Dec. 23, 1871, (*Jan.* 4, 1872).

MY DEAR JOHN,

I hope you received my last letter all right, as although I believe letters are safely carried to their destination, newspapers suffer a different fate ; those not in the official list are destroyed, and those which are, have to pass through a censorship at the frontier before continuing their journey, and sometimes lose a column or two. To-day we received *The Times* of Thursday, the 28th December, and on the eighth page, end of third column, there was a large black patch, obliterating something, at the end of which I could only read *Mall Gazette,* thus depriving the poor *Pall Mall* of its christian name, from which paper *The Times* had copied the article in question, whatever it may happen to have been. With true feminine curiosity, Louise, assisted by Bateson, began to consider how they could circumvent the enemy and restore the legibility of the print: but all in vain, the more they tried to get the Satanic colour off, the faster it stuck, and the blacker it became. So having given it up as hopeless, and not wishing to be beaten, Louise wants you to cut it out and send it in a letter, and thus *do* the censor at the frontier.

Here we are as you see by the dates of my letter living a double existence. As English men and women we have had our Christmas-day, and our New Year's-day; but as temporary Russians we are still in the year 1871, and are going in for more roast beef and plum pudding next Saturday—the *Russian* Christmas-day; the classical reason for our double jollity being that the calendar in use in Russia is the Julian or Greek, which is twelve days behind the Gregorian or Latin, so that as we are now situated, I have the advantage of being twelve days more your junior than you thought I was.

But now a truce to fun : let's to business and be serious, as Money says, when nobody is listening to him. Pomerania ; that's were we are supposed to be on our journey travelling from Berlin to the Prussian frontier of Eydkuhnen, and longing to be the other side of it, at Wierzbolow, our first Russian town : but we have yet several hundred miles to get there, so I must "jot" down a little by the way. Just as we started from Berlin we made another acquaintance besides "Roger," an officer in the Blues, height, 6-ft. 4-in., wrapped up in a splendid Astracan "Shuba," and to whom I had previously called Chambers' attention, as being a magnificent Russian. It seems he had previously travelled with Isenbeck, and added materially to the pleasure of the saloon party as far as Wilna. Our Guardsman is a perfect marvel, he speaks nine living languages— Russian included—and has travelled over pretty nearly the whole of this world, occupying all his " leave " in so doing; and if he can only get " leave " in the next, there is no knowing where he would not go.

Now, I have no doubt hundreds of English railway directors have travelled on these German lines and if they are not deprived of the means of observation, they must have noticed many little things—small in their way—but calculated to be of great service and convenience to railway travellers, which they might have very easily introduced on their own railways. *Here's one*,—In this North Prussian carriage there is a pasteboard card, about one foot square, headed " Fahrplanmassige " (travelling plan regulations), and underneath, " Aufenthaltszeiten " (stopping times), and it proceeds to give you for the train you are in, its time of arrival at the stations, time of departure, difference carried out in another column as stopping time, and all times between 6 p.m. and 6 a.m., have a blue shade painted across them, leaving them quite legible, but intended to show you that those are night times, without adding the p.m. or a.m., which sometimes carried through two or three days and nights, confuses you. It is well known that the Jews begin their day at 6. a.m., and their night at 6 p.m. each lasting twelve hours. The recurrence to this old mode of dividing the day and night, and the darkening of the hours indicating the latter, is a great improvement on our railway time tables. On *another* side you are informed where there is to be a Table d'hôte, and other species of refreshment, what are the " Schlafvorrichtungen," or sleeping arrangements in the carriages, and the " Zollabfertigung," or revision of luggage in the Custom Houses, besides other information, valuable to the traveller on the line.

By Jove! Here we are at Dirschau, a town in ancient Poland, and crossing the frozen Vistula, a river familiar to my school days, and now we are going over its magnificent bridge, half a mile long, leaving Dantzig on our left, where the deals come from; De'il take it! as on opening the window to look out, there came such a cold blast from its gulf; if *he* had it, he might warm it up a bit; and now we look out for Marienburg, and its Palace of the Ancient Grand Masters of the Teutonic Order, who nearly had their own house about their ears on one occasion when they were besieged in it. The *Meisters Remter*, or chapter house of the order, in which assemblies of the order were held and foreign ambassadors received, for they were great swells in those times, rests on a *single* pillar of granite in the centre. The Poles, while besieging the City in 1410, endeavoured to aim a cannon ball so as to shoot away this pillar, and overwhelm at one blow beneath the ruins, the Grand Master and all his Knights, whom they knew from the information of a deserter, to be at the time assembled in conclave. *The ball missed its aim, but lodged in a corner of the chimney where it still remains.*

Königsberg, once the capital of Prussia-proper, and *now* third city in the Prussian dominions. There, in the *Schlosskirche*, Frederick, Elector of Brandenburg, in 1701, placed the crown on his own head, assuming the title of Frederick I. King of Prussia, just as the present King William of Prussia, and now Emperor of Germany, is reported to have done when he came to the Throne, and coronetted himself by the Divine will, following the example of his ancestor. I am informed there is a considerable quantity of amber found all along the coast near Königsberg, and this is how they get it. The high winds throw up a vast accumulation of seaweed. The amberfishers go up to their necks, provided with nets, by which they draw the weeds to land. The amber accumulates in the lower beds of the sea sand extending under the Baltic, and when the storms bear up the amber earth, the amber is carried to the surface.

Now we are traversing the frontier of Prussia and Russia, and when we get to Wilna I shall have something to say about Napoleon and his calamitous invasion of Russia in 1812; but although these broad flat plains on which we now gaze, covered with snow, are not very interesting, there is a talk among us all, that it may not be very long before they will have the attention of all Europe attracted to them, because here Prussia and Russia meet, and their broad and flat expanses of land must be the future battle ground, if ever these two enormous empires close in deadly conflict, which pray God avert. We have seen how the Prussian officers, lately invested with the Russian order of Knights of St. George, were received by the Emperor Alexander at St. Petersburg, and subsequently at Moscow, and with what hearty good will the Emperor of all the Russias has addressed them on all occasions, winding up with his paternal speech at the banquet; and as long as His Majesty lives I trust nothing will occur to change his present good feeling towards the Germans; but "here's the rub." The Czarewitch is known to be anti-German, and from what I learn here, does not smother his sentiments. He is married to the Danish Princess Dagmar, sister to our Princess of Wales, and in this country, the Czar, when he comes to the throne, is an autocrat, and declares war or makes peace on his own responsibility, and my observation (limited, certainly, but, as far as it goes, trustworthy) is that the Russians are beginning to be jealous of the Prussians and their late doings, as the Prussians seem to be giving themselves " airs " everywhere, which creates an antagonistic feeling in the persons " aired," and is not calculated to inspire them with a peaceful feeling towards their " airers ; "—so do not let us be so sure that the French people and the French press are insane, in imagining that some day or other the Russians and

French may not become allies; but here is the *bonâ fide* frontier at last, and we step out on Russian soil at Wierzbolow. Bravo, you Russian Tartars! I like the look of you! " Good buffet, and plenty of time for refreshment!" I like that, too; so does Louise, and so does Bateson, who, like Dickens' Marchioness, "liked her meals in quiet and plenty of 'em." " Change carriages, passports and luggage examined." All right, we have only nine large portmanteaus and boxes in the van, and twelve little parcels in the carriage, which have altogether cost to St. Petersburg a mere trifle of £.18 or so in excess of the allowance; but I would not be so mean as to say that Loui has had anything to do with this *limited* " baggage;" however, business first and pleasure afterwards, so we at once go about our luggage, and then pay our warmest respects to the buffet. But now, before I in imagination go into that buffet, I will perform my first duty towards the Russians, by suggesting to any English custom-house officer, that *here*, in what our true born Briton might call an outlandish place, he would learn a good lesson as to how his duty ought to be performed. First of all, everything in Russia is colossal, and yet convenient, and we find that in a spacious douane, surrounded by a circular counter, numbered in divisions, without any hurry, bustle, or confusion, all our luggage is taken by the porters to a certain definite place, corresponding in duplicate to our numbered register ticket; there the van luggage is deposited, and to the same place all the small parcels find their way, the officer on duty specifies to his Douaniers what his requirements are, and, finding that we are a party of British subjects travelling for pleasure, and not for trade, he deals most gently with our wardrobes, barely regarding even, some new ball dresses, which Louise had had separately packed by the milliner, fresh from her establishment, in large deal boxes.

The gentlemen of our party, after acknowledging the courtesy of the Russian Douane officer, by saluting him with their raised hats, all wended their way to the "refreshmenting department," as poor Charles Dickens called it, and found there yet another example for our English, "Mugby Junction." Half-a-dozen hot viands to choose from, accompanied by soup, coffee, or wine, and all of the best quality and description, served at a moment's notice, on table-cloths white as snow, with most attentive and respectful waiters; add to this lavatories, with the requisite accompaniments of soap, towels, &c., and I leave you to judge of what has been talked about as barbarous Russia.

Here we are, on our first introduction at a frontier station, finding more civilization than has happened to my lot in many an old country through which I have travelled, and you will find that when you have received other letters from me, describing our future progress, and stay, at all events at St. Petersburg, they will contain similar continued experiences, supporting our first agreeable impressions.

Wierzbolow, I find, is 560 miles from the capital, where we shall arrive to-morrow evening, so we are beginning to be near the end. And now time is up, and we must get ourselves into Russian railway quarters for the first time. Let me count how many we are: Louise, myself, and Bateson, Money, Chambers, Isenbeck, and the giant of the blues; and now let me next make a survey of a first-class railway carriage; here it is before me, and it appears to be something entirely novel. It has two ends and a middle. Well,

B

so have most things ; but how are they arranged ? At each end there is a compartment, for say, five sitters, but comfortably containing only three passengers, and the middle has four small square compartments (two on each side of the centre passage), large enough for one comfortably to curl up and sleep in although evidently intended for more. Well, now outside, just in advance of the end compartments, there are doors by which you enter a cross passage, leading to a centre passage, which takes you to your respective compartments, so that by securing for Louise, her maid, and myself, one end compartment, and the others taking unto themselves the four centre small compartments, we leave the other end for stray passengers on the way, or others getting in at Wierzbolow. There are two stoves, one of which is fixed in the interior division of each of the end compartments, so that half the stove is in the carriage, and the other half in the cross passage, and as the temperature was about 70° Fahrenheit on entering, we began to think we should not, at all events, suffer from cold on our journey.

If you can follow this plan, so difficult to describe, you will perceive that our party were all, as it were, together under one roof, and that we could pay each other visits in our respective cabins, as our lumbering, old, rolling, but still comfortable carriage, put me much in mind of a steamer of the olden time ; and its wheels, as they rolled over the frozen rails, sounded just like the paddles beating against the waves.

Louise strongly objected to be stifled with heat in Russia, where she had expected to have met her fate by frost, and requested me to address myself to the "stove-keeper," who accompanies every first-class carriage, to reduce it by machinery which they have for that dresses, which Louise had had separately packed by the milliner, fresh from her establishment, in large deal boxes.

The gentlemen of our party, after acknowledging the courtesy of the Russian Douane officer, by saluting him with their raised hats, all wended their way to the "refreshmenting department," as poor Charles Dickens called it, and found there yet another example for our English, "Mugby Junction." Half-a-dozen hot viands to choose from, accompanied by soup, coffee, or wine, and all of the best quality and description, served at a moment's notice, on table-cloths white as snow, with most attentive and respectful waiters; add to this lavatories, with the requisite accompaniments of soap, towels, &c., and I leave you to judge of what has been talked about as barbarous Russia.

Here we are, on our first introduction at a frontier station, finding more civilization than has happened to my lot in many an old country through which I have travelled, and you will find that when you have received other letters from me, describing our future progress, and stay, at all events at St. Petersburg, they will contain similar continued experiences, supporting our first agreeable impressions.

Wierzbolow, I find, is 560 miles from the capital, where we shall arrive to-morrow evening, so we are beginning to be near the end. And now time is up, and we must get ourselves into Russian railway quarters for the first time. Let me count how many we are: Louise, myself, and Bateson, Money, Chambers, Isenbeck, and the giant of the blues; and now let me next make a survey of a first-class railway carriage; here it is before me, and it appears to be something entirely novel. It has two ends and a middle. Well,

B

so have most things; but how are they arranged? At each end there is a compartment, for say, five sitters, but comfortably containing only three passengers, and the middle has four small square compartments (two on each side of the centre passage), large enough for one comfortably to curl up and sleep in although evidently intended for more. Well, now outside, just in advance of the end compartments, there are doors by which you enter a cross passage, leading to a centre passage, which takes you to your respective compartments, so that by securing for Louise, her maid, and myself, one end compartment, and the others taking unto themselves the four centre small compartments, we leave the other end for stray passengers on the way, or others getting in at Wierzbolow. There are two stoves, one of which is fixed in the interior division of each of the end compartments, so that half the stove is in the carriage, and the other half in the cross passage, and as the temperature was about 70° Fahrenheit on entering, we began to think we should not, at all events, suffer from cold on our journey.

If you can follow this plan, so difficult to describe, you will perceive that our party were all, as it were, together under one roof, and that we could pay each other visits in our respective cabins, as our lumbering, old, rolling, but still comfortable carriage, put me much in mind of a steamer of the olden time; and its wheels, as they rolled over the frozen rails, sounded just like the paddles beating against the waves.

Louise strongly objected to be stifled with heat in Russia, where she had expected to have met her fate by frost, and requested me to address myself to the "stove-keeper," who accompanies every first-class carriage, to reduce it by machinery which they have for that purpose, and so I "unearthed" our Russian fireman from a corner of the cross-passage, in which he had doubled himself up for a nap; and now began a series of amusing signs and symbols, which continued, with varied intermission, between this interesting old man and myself during the next twenty-four hours of our journey. He was a character in his way, and seemed to be a Russian originally from the far interior of Siberia, of the Tartar race—brawny and muscular, with high cheek-bones, small bright eyes, terribly shaggy hair, and a face as broad as it was long—a complete parallelogram. We soon got friends after arranging the stove to Louise's satisfaction, and with the help of a Russian vocabulary I entered into conversation with him, and asked him about his age. Answer: His 10 fingers held up six times and finishing with seven more —67. Are you married? Answer: Pointing to the wedding-ring finger and running round it three times. Why, three wives? Answer: Broad grin and several affirmative shakes of the head. How many children? Answer: 19 fingers held up, one hand after the other, and then three fingers gently and mournfully doubled down—16 alive and three dead. And so we continued, I racking my brain, and sometimes going to Louise for inspiration as to how I was to convey to him my symbolic questions, which took me some time to invent, and then more time to express. Poor old fellow! We treated him to a "go" of our fine old Cognac out of the picnic basket, and his wistful looks towards it when he came for directions about the stove, which he frequently did, induced one or two more on the journey; but the climax of all occurred when we were nearing our destination, when I procured about a dozen small Russian silver pieces, and then, concealing them in my left hand, I doled them out to him in our cabin one after the other. Louise says she shall never forget the expression of his face as I proceeded. When animated with a smile it became slightly broader than it was long, but, when the pieces of silver repeated themselves towards the last, the broadness of his face became most ludicrous, and even ridiculous, to behold; his eyes brightened, and his mouth extended itself to unusual dimensions. At length a revulsion of feeling came over him, and brushing away a tear, he caught up both our hands, kissed them, retired to his little den, and we shall probably see him no more.

550 miles from St. Petersburg, at "Kowno," where on the 22nd June, 1812, the French army crossed the Niemen on their advance to Moscow, and some rising ground on the opposite bank is still called Napoleon's Hill. The town of Kowno was occupied by a large *corps d'armée*, and suffered considerably. The remnants of the army recrossed the river at the same spot on the 13th December, in a very bad state of discipline. There is a monument existing commemorating this retreat, and bearing the following inscription in Russian, which, translated, is as follows:—" In 1812 Russia was invaded by an army numbering 700,000 men. The army recrossed the frontier numbering 70,000 !!"

441 miles from St. Petersburg, at "Wilna," occupied by the French on the 28th June, 1812. It had been evacuated by the Russians during the night. The Emperor Napoleon occupied the Episcopal Palace, the rooms which the Emperor Alexander had left the previous day. The country all along here is covered with snow, so I cannot form an idea as to its cultivation, but the villages are few and far between, and those do not exhibit any high degree of prosperity. They are mostly

composed of wood, somewhat resembling, only in a poorer degree, the Swiss mountain châlets. Birds are scarce, not liking, probably, to face the deep snow. We have only seen two magpies for miles; but as the old couplet says,

> "One magpie is sorrow, two mirth,
> Three a wedding, and four a birth."

Our two are symbolical of what is going on inside our carriage, where we are the jolliest of parties; Louise holds her levées, when the gentlemen are invited by her to our cabin, where the floor is cheerfully occupied by those who cannot otherwise be accommodated, and cigars and cigarettes are the order of the day, combined with pleasant instructive conversation by travelled men, interspersed with merry stories. I won't repeat what pretty things are said by our fellow travellers to Louise, but by general acclamation she is declared to be the life and soul of the party, and a splendid traveller.

Between stations separated by long distances, we amuse ourselves with the contents of the picnic basket, and having Liebeg's essence, and Fortnum and Mason's compressed beef tea, with other delicacies, our Etna boils up some water, and we get a capital entertainment in the Swiss Family Robinson style. Our cabins are now kept by our old friend (if he will allow me the privilege of calling him so; as they say at public meetings), at a delicious temperature, but when we issue forth at a station, we all don our complete suit of furs, as the air is nipping cold, but full of oxygen, and ozone, as the country is overlaid for hundreds, and even thousands of miles, with its wintry covering of snow, and we are warned by a notice not to put our heads out of the little window of our cabin, which is only a foot square, as "*Cette imprudence pourrait avoir des conséquences graves.*" But with our splendid shubas, caps, boots, and gloves, it is impossible even to feel a shiver, with many more degrees of frost than we have had yet.

We get most delicious coffee at the buffets, and still more delicious tea, served in tumblers for the gentlemen, and cups for the ladies, with milk, that the Russians are not yet sufficiently civilised to adulterate with unwholesome materials, and notice is given you of the starting of the train by three bells first pealing outside the station, and repeated by an official at the refreshment-room door, rung successfully at intervals of a few minutes—the first a notice, the second a warning, and the third, we're off. All along the line the men live in wood huts, which are all numbered outside with white paint, starting from the capital, so you can count off your approximation to the end of your journey as you go along. And now the numbers are gradually diminishing, until at length St. Petersburg bursts upon our view, with its colossal public buildings, its gorgeous palaces, and churches with gilded cupolas; Sleighs with fast-trotting horses are awaiting us, into which we get with alacrity, leaving our luggage to the commissionaire of the hotel to bring after us, and we drive off at the rate of twelve miles an hour over the frozen snow to the Hôtel de Russie, where we find, as we ordered by telegram, warm baths, comfortably heated rooms, a dinner *à la Russe*, all awaiting our kind attention; more of which anon.

   I remain, MY DEAR JOHN,
     Your affectionate brother,
       R. RICHARDSON-GARDNER.

HÔTEL DE RUSSIE,
ST. PETERSBURG,
29*th* Dec. 1871–10*th* Jan. 1872.

MY DEAR JOHN,

I think I bade you " Adieu " in my last as our sleighs dashed up to the door of this hotel, and we all dismounted, to find everything prepared for our reception, including a *Dîner-à-la-Russe*, served Russian fashion; but as we have already received the hospitality of our Russian friends by assisting (as the French say) at more than one entertainment of that kind on a more elaborate scale, I will reserve a description of that important ceremony until I come to such events in the natural course of things, and now only describe our domicile to you as we find ourselves inhabiting it.

We are located on the *belle étage* of this hotel, which being the first hotel in St. Petersburg, is probably the best in all Russia. Our suite of rooms is, as it were, a little house all within itself, as we have a reception room about sixteen feet high, and large in proportion, elegantly, and even sumptuously, furnished; ditto bedroom, servants' rooms, and an entrance lobby, with front door and bell, where visitors disrobe themselves of their huge fur shubas and overboots, and where our Russian dragoman is in attendance to assist when we are "at.home." We have two excellent lithographs of the Prince of Wales in our windows, of which we procured twenty copies before leaving London to present to our friends here, who are delighted to receive them. They are excellent likenesses by Maclure and Macdonald. We had a capital letter from James the other day, in which he said he should be prepared to hear from us, that, "In Russia cold was not cold, snow was not snow, and that ice was not ice, except in the shape of ice creams." But I can assure you, paradoxical as it may seem, that neither I nor Louise, who is peculiarly sensitive to climate, have felt a shiver since we have been here. Our rooms are kept at an invariable temperature of 65 degrees Fahrenheit; the windows are all double and airtight, so thus there are no draughts. When the front door opens, as the passages are all heated alike, there is no rush of cold air, and when we go out we wear all the warm furs that I have previously described to you. As you wish me to give you all details with regard to our sojourn in Russia—a country so little known, and not half appreciated—I will comply with your request by giving you, to begin with, the price of our rooms as 12 roubles (equal to 33s. a day), taken for three or four weeks certain.

I do not say Russia is a cheap country to live in, either for native or foreigner; on the contrary, I must admit at once that it is very dear, as there are comparatively only two classes in the country—the nobles, or wealthy landowners, and the working classes, or peasants. The first are, for the most part rich, profuse, and reckless—extravagant, sometimes even to folly, and totally regardless of the prices paid by them for anything that they want, and which, when required, must be had irrespective of cost. The second, until lately absolute serfs, have not yet attained even to the comforts of life beyond the natural requirements of existence. For the first, St. Petersburg has become the emporium of all the refinements and luxuries that not only the length and breadth of Europe can produce, but to which Asia has also largely contributed, so that, whether it be summer or winter, fruits of the rarest quality, vegetables, and flowers, and all the delicacies in season, or out of season, can equally well be procured for the bit of paper stamped with the Imperial arms and Crown, and representing roubles, more or less. Under these circumstances, "Put money in thy purse" when thou comest to Russia, and I will back the Russians to empty it for you; "'Twas mine, 'tis his, and has been slave to thousands."

Well, now, where shall I begin? My head is full of the thousand and one things I have to tell you about, and the very multiplicity of them is my difficulty. We are in St. Michael's Square, in the very heart of St. Petersburg, with the Nobility Club adjoining us, and the splendid Corinthian Palace of the Grand Duchess Helen opposite us; and as I get up to consider and look out of the window, and wonder how I am to begin, my attention is arrested, or distracted, by the Grand Duchess's seven dogs, just let out for their morning's gambol into the square, to disport themselves in the snow. They are playing with an old hat, and the "little wee dog" has got inside, and the others are bowling him over and over, and enjoying the fun.

I have made up my mind that I must take my text from the Admiralty—not Childers', or Goschen's, but someone's with a precious long name, which I fear to write, and endeavour from that *point d'appui* to give you a slight idea of the topography of the town.

The Admiralty is an oblong square, with its back to the river Neva on its north side, and its front of half an English mile in length on the south side, facing a large square or place bearing its name. Its two sides or ends are each 650 English feet long. In the middle part of this edifice is the principal entrance, over which floats, as it were, a light and graceful spire, centred in which is a clock. Now, consider yourself located in this clock, and I will endeavour to direct its long hand so that it may point out to you the great town in front of it, and its short hand the lesser town behind it.

By making the long hand point at a right angle to the face of the clock, over the Admiralty "Ploschad" or square, it will shew you a street in a direct line with itself, stretching straight away for a distance of about two miles. This street is called Gorokhovaia Street. The long hand must now bear a little to the right, and it will point straight down another street, about two and a half miles long, which street is called Vosnesenski Prospekt. Again, it bears as much to the left of the centre as it did to the right, and it will point straight down the largest and longest street of the three. This is the principal street of St. Petersburg, half as wide again as Regent Street, and about three miles long, and is called the Nevski Prospekt. These streets start from the Admiralty place, not far from each other, but, by bearing away from one another, form themselves into the shape of a fan, of which the clock might be the handle, so that if you place yourself at the furtherest end of either of them, you would still have a view of the clock, and from the clock you can see to their remotest end. All the other streets are, without exception, broad and convenient, blind alleys and narrow lanes being wholly unknown. The cross streets even would be thought, in most continental towns, to be quite spacious enough for main streets.

Surrounding and contiguous to the Admiralty Ploschad, we have a succession of palaces, noble buildings, and monuments. Among them are the Winter Palace, the residence of the Emperor and his Court during winter. The huge pile is four stories high, or about 80 feet, the frontage is about 455 feet in length, and the breadth 350 feet. The Hermitage, a grand museum, erected in the Greek style, and which for elegance, purity of architectural form, and for the beauty, as well as for the costliness of the materials employed, has scarcely an equal in Europe. It forms a parallelogram 515 feet by 375, and is approached by a noble vestibule, supported by ten immense Caryatides of grey granite, measuring 22 feet with their pedestals. It is connected with the palace by an arch in the form of a bridge. The Isaac Cathedral, dedicated to St. Isaac, of Dalmatia, a building of grand proportions, and of a simple but lofty style of architecture, with noble porticoes, supported by huge Monolith pillars of Finland granite, 60 feet high, and seven feet diameter, said to be the largest Monoliths in the world. The Hôtel de l'Etat-Major, the Foreign Office, the War Office, the Senate, and the Synod, the Statues of Peter the Great, and Alexander the First. As I do not intend to enter into long descriptions, I can only say that wherever the long hand of the clock can point on the south side of the Neva, it could not cover one hundred yards of ground without encountering marble palaces, churches, monuments, and public buildings, which must be seen to be appreciated.

And now, if we suppose the short hand to be pointing towards the north, right across the river Neva, it will show you the Fortress and Cathedral of St. Peter and St. Paul, the Exchange, the Academy of Sciences, the Academy of Arts, the School of Marine Cadets, the School of Mines, &c. The most interesting features of the interior of those buildings and churches, I shall touch upon in the course of my epistle.

The first thing to do when you arrive here is to engage a "Dragoman," who can speak your language and his own; and the second thing is to know how to hail a "Droshki Sleigh." Well, we have done the first by engaging a native, of the name of Ivan Michael Timofeieff, during our stay in the country, at a salary of three roubles a day, and all expenses paid. (N.B., three copecks are about one penny, 100 copecks make one rouble, and one rouble is two shillings and ninepence; this is all the information you require about the Russian coinage). As Ivan is likely to go with us to Moscow, Smolensk, Wilna, and Warsaw, and will necessarily have to be occasionally mentioned, you might like to make his acquaintance, so I beg to inform you that Ivan is a true born Russian, 42 years of age, exactly five feet nothing high in his boots (I measured him by stratagem), is married to a very tall woman, and has a family of six children. He was born, and continued to be a serf until emancipated by the present Emperor Alexander's ukase, was several years Chasseur of the American Embassy, more especially when Cassius Clay was minister, speaks English pretty well, Russian I suppose better. Although a very small man, he has a wonderful presence, and orders about the big Droshki men, and porters, with a most distinguished air of superiority, and what's more they obey him. They have christened him John the Terrible, after one of Russia's most autocratic despots. His success comes, I think from his intellectual head, which is immense for his size, in fact, the whole contour of his person reminds me, on a small scale, of the great Emperor Napoleon, so much so that when he draws himself up to give his commands, I honour him with the designation of that great general. By means of copecks judiciously administered, he can always get the guardians of public places to give us good positions, to see what is to be seen, and when these guardians are beyond the reach of Ivan's bribes he accosts them with his hat off and bowing to the ground, saying, "An Englis nobblemann and nobbleladye presents their complements," &c., &c. Oh, Ivan! Ivan! He knows everything and everybody, or pretends to, which is much the same, and he is so clever and has such a good memory, that if ever he tells me a "white one" he remembers it, and although I occasionally lay a trap for him I can't catch him. He is an honest little fellow in money matters, and that is a great virtue *here*, perhaps I might say *anywhere* with men of his class, or perhaps with other classes too; so that if any of our friends come to Russia and want a dragoman they could not do better than write to Ivan Michael Timofeieff, Hotel Klée, St. Petersburg, and he will engage rooms at the hotel or meet them at the railway, or do any other commission that may be required; and now I have done Ivan a good turn I will proceed. Where was I? Oh! the droshki sleigh, and how to hail it; convert the final P of his worship into K, pronounce it as one word quickly, rolling the R, and you get my elegant invention of a Russian word *hisworshik*, which will bring you a droshki sleigh in a moment, and you will be surprised at the progress you have made in the language. But you will say, what is a droshki sleigh? It is a cab, not a four-wheeler or a hansom, but a little box, which is the droshki, fitted on to two slides, which is the sleigh, altogether about 2½ feet from the ground. The seat is very narrow, and can only be intended for one person to sit on, and the driver perches himself in front of you on a curious apparatus in a semicircular form, with one leg in a receptacle and one dangling out over the side, with a great horse " displaying immense symmetry of bone" dragging you along at a tremendous pace, whose tail is considerably higher than your head. If you are a small party of two you may still manage, after some experience, to sit in the droshki sleigh by holding on by each other; but it is attended with some risk, especially round the corners, until you are Russianised, and consequently expert.

Our square is just out of the principal street, Nevski Prospekt, about 1½ mile down from the clock, and now let us step out into the Nevski and see what is going on. Fortunately, there is a large, two-horsed droshki sleigh, licensed to carry two or more, so I hail him with *hisworshik*, which brings him to us immediately, and as this is all the Russian I know Ivan bargains with him for a drive round the town per hour. (By-the-bye, I must omit from all things dear the droshkis, they are the only reasonable things in Russia.) We have two good, black horses, and they take us down the Nevski at a rattling pace over the snow, the road being wide enough for a division into two roads, one for updriving and one for downdriving; and now I will mention a few

of the following objects of interest as we go along:—
The Palace of the Czarevitch, fortunately meeting the Princess Dagmar just coming out in her sleigh, who looked so well and returned our respectful salute. You may always know the Czaritsa's (the Empress's) carriage and the Czarievna's (the Crown Princess's) carriage by their Cossack footmen being special to them. The Alexander Nevski Monastery and Church, the archiepiscopal seat of the metropolitan of St. Petersburg, the Taurida Palace, built by Catherine II. in 1783, and given by her to Field Marshal Potemkin after he had conquered the Crimea and received the submission of the King of Georgia; the Prosbragenski Church, which belongs to one of the oldest regiments of guards, founded by Peter the Great, and is adorned within and without with trophies taken from conquered nations. The railing that surrounds the churchyard is formed of Turkish and French cannon, looped together by large chains gracefully twined, producing a very pleasing effect. The Palace de Justice, where justice is now administered on the basis of open trial by jury, a reform which came into operation at Moscow and St. Petersburg in 1865, during the present Emperor's reign. A great mansion, where the Emperor's servants and their families are lodged. The Emperor employs the unprecedented number of 2,000 servants, half of whom are always on duty, the other half off, and their families are all lodged under one roof. What would Sir Charles Dilke say to this small establishment? The New Arsenal; and then we come to the Summer Garden, the Hyde Park of St. Petersburg. In former days the sons and daughters of Russian merchants and tradesmen, dressed in their best apparel, assembled in this garden

on Whit-Monday to choose partners for life; but the custom is now almost obsolete. At the entrance of the garden, facing the river, is a chapel, dedicated to the patron saint of the Emperor, marking the spot where he stood when his life was attempted by Karakozoff in 1866. The chapel was raised by public subscription, and is therefore a monument of the love and sympathy of the Russian people, to whom the present Czar has much endeared himself. I give you the story of this attempt as it has been communicated to me.

It seems there was a peasant, who had intended to cross the frozen river Neva, to proceed to the Cathedral of St. Peter and St. Paul to attend the service there; but, finding the ice breaking up, he changed his mind, and was directing his steps to another cathedral, that of Kazan, on this side of the river, when, observing a crowd standing near the gate of the Summer Garden in order to catch a glimpse of the Czar, he stopped too, and got himself into a good place. Presently the Czar came out of the garden, accompanied by his daughter, when the peasant felt himself rudely pushed by some one on his right, and looking round, was just in time to knock up the uplifted arm of the assassin Karakozoff, whose finger was on the trigger of his pistol, and the ball of which thus passed harmlessly into the air instead of into the body of the Czar. The assassin was seized, and the peasant, frightened out of his life, took to his heels. With the celebrated General Todleben in pursuit, he was soon overtaken, led to the Palace, and presented to the Emperor and Empress as the peasant who had saved the Emperor's life. They both embraced him, and the Czar then and there proclaimed him hereafter as a noble of the land. Special emissaries were immediately despatched for the new noble's wife, who lived in a house which we have seen, and is situated in a street leading out of "Sadovaia" Street, and called "Apraxin Pereulok," to acquaint her with her good fortune, and to take her by order of the Czar to the Palace. The poor woman was busy preparing her own and her husband's dinner against his return, and when the officers entered was terribly frightened, believing her husband had fallen into some trouble and had been sent to prison, and they were come to fetch her also. However, she was soon undeceived, but the orders were she was to return with them immediately, so the noble lady was not even allowed to "tidy herself," but was carried straight off to the Empress, where we must leave the two women of high and low degree to feel that "touch of nature which makes the whole world kin." The peasant and his wife now rank among the nobility of Russia, and the peasant is an officer in the Emperor's service.

And now we drive along the Court quay and the English quay for a distance of two or three miles, passing palaces and magnificent mansions facing the river, which are occupied by the Grand Dukes and other scions of the Royal House, besides the Russian nobles, and wealthy landowners, bankers, and merchants. The Grand Duke Constantine's palace is of marble, and there is a beautiful new palace just built for the Grand Duke Vladimir, the Czar's second son, and so on, with a never ending variety of grand architecture of all styles and ages. While we are fighting at home about a design for our law courts, why do not some of our architects run over here and copy a style if they can't invent it.

Over the Neva, frozen three feet deep, driven in our

sleighs, with our horses at a gallop, there's a sensation for you! It was for us, and Louise, although a little alarmed at first at being actually on the surface of a great river in a chariot, soon became familiarised with it, and would have another turn. Back again, over a bridge of elegant iron arches, on magnificent granite piers, which was erected by the late Czar Nicholas, and cost a very large sum of money. The poor people here think that it is in the power of the Czar to print as many bank notes as he likes for the use of himself and his friends, so Ivan informs us, that it is commonly said among them that the bridge only cost the Czar 40lbs. of old rags. And now across the Admiralty Place, past your friend the clock, and down the Nevski to our hotel, having seen more marvellous modern architecture than you can possibly see in any other city in Europe, or any other two put together.

The Russians date their civilisation from Peter the Great, and worship his memory; and well they may, as this great place has been all built from its foundations in 168 years, St. Petersburg being founded by Peter in 1703, and converted by his indomitable perseverance from a swamp into a palatial city, now containing a vast population, the Czar himself superintending the works in person, and dwelling in a small cottage, which we have this day visited.

The day after our drive, we took a walk, and found at every step something to interest us. I know no place where your attention is so unceasingly occupied by ordinary sights in the streets as at St. Petersburg, and what is it which strikes us first? Why, the great number of shrines of Saints, which are constantly meeting your eye, and the marvellous devotion shown by the people as they pass them; not one but takes his hat off and crosses himself, bowing three times as he does so to the Shrine which engages his attention, and they do this not only when immediately near, but even in passing at the end of a cross street, and they see a Shrine in the distance, so that one is constantly wondering what the people can be bowing to; but, remember, that is all done from perfect devotion to their faith, an example of which we witnessed on the Russian Christmas-day in their Cathedral, and which I shall describe to you further on.

One curious little incident occurred to me during our perambulation. I must tell you that during the election at Windsor, there was a queer old fellow, an Eton College waterman, of the name of Cannon, more familiarly known as "Sparrow," who never missed attending any of my political meetings, and when I had been holding forth for some time, he invariably brought me a glass of ale, saying, "Colonel, you can't give me one, but I can treat you," and I always accepted it with much satisfaction. Well, poor old Sparrow had a little wife, a very tidy, neat, little woman, who had, of course, seen better days, and her peculiarity was to always stop in the street when she saw me coming a long way off, and commence a series of bows, which seemed as if they would never come to an end. Of course I always spoke to her, and asked kindly after her beneficent husband. Now, crossing a street here, I came suddenly upon a little woman, the exact counterpart of Mrs. Sparrow; and there she was bowing away just like my little old friend. Well, with what Mr. Pickwick would call, my "Native politeness," and my Windsor experiences, I forgot for the moment where I was; so up I went to the little old woman, and said, "How dy'e do, mum? How is Sparrow?" when she crossed herself three times, and not even noticed me; and then I remembered I had never seen Mrs. Sparrow do the one or neglect the other, and the consciousness of the little old woman being a Russian, and a Devotee, immediately recurred to my mind, and I sidled off as best I could.

And, so, farewell until my next,

Your affectionate brother,

R. RICHARDSON-GARDNER.

HÔTEL DE RUSSIE,

ST. PETERSBURG,

1–13*th January*, 1872.

MY DEAR JOHN,

At length we have both got into the year 1872. This is New Year's day in Russia, on which occasion the Czar of all the Russias holds a grand levée in the Winter Palace, at which all the Diplomatic Corps, the great Ministers of State, the heads of the different departments, the highest naval and military officers, and the grandees of all kinds from his immense dominions are present, to do homage to the Chief of the State and the head of the Church, and a very splendid ceremony it is. You are aware that we had some excellent introductions to Russians of position at St. Petersburg, who have done everything in their power to make our visit agreeable to us, and it was suggested that as we had both been presented at our own court, if our names were sent to Prince Gortchakoff by the English representative at this court, His Majesty the Emperor would probably receive me, and her Majesty the Empress receive Louise at a presentation; and further that through the influential friends we possess, it might be followed by an invitation to the grand new year's ball which takes place next week at the Palace. Well, all this has come about, as I had the honour of being presented to His Majesty the Emperor this morning, and was thus enabled to witness the magnificent and gorgeous state by which he is surrounded.

Louise is to be presented to the Empress at the ball, to which we have both received invitations.

As you would probably like to know something of the state kept up in the northern capital of Europe, I will give you a short description of how things appeared to me. I left my hotel in my uniform of deputy-lieutenant, and proceeded to the Palace, alighting at the entrance for the Diplomatic Corps, where I met our representative, who is acting as Chargé d'affaires, until the arrival of Lord Augustus Loftus, who is the lately appointed Ambassador, and we proceeded to the reception room appointed for us, after which we were eventually ushered into the throne-room where the presentations take place, passing by on our way, a magnificent suite of rooms, adorned by pictures of the reigning Royal Family, and other rare works of art. There I had the honour of being presented to, among many others, Prince Dolgorouki (grand master of the ceremonies), Count Schuvaloff, and the man of all others I much wished to see, Prince Gortchakoff (the prime minister of the Czar), and of course a European celebrity—his latest feat being the half-persuading and half-frightening the western powers—England in particular—with Gladstone at its head, into annulling that part of the Black Sea treaty for which England's gold was expended, and England's blood was shed in the Crimean war.

After waiting some time, a grand cortège approached. and the procession, reaching the whole length of an immense ball-room, ushered into our room their Imperial Majesties the Czar and the Empress, accompanied by the Crown Princess (the Princess Dagmar, sister to the Princess of Wales), with the Crown Prince, the Grand Duke Vladimir, the Princess Mary, the Grand Dukes

Nicholas and Constantine, and the remaining members of the Royal family at St. Petersburg. Preceding them came the officers of state, then an army of grand chamberlains, and chamberlains in court dress, elegantly overlaid with gold embroidery, and bearing wands of office, and after their Majesties came a bevy of beauty, consisting of about fifty of the ladies of the court in attendance on the Empress, wearing the rarest jewels and gems. The mode of presentation here is diffcrent to that adopted at our Court, and I think very much in favour of the Court at St. Petersburg. The Czar and the Empress both proceed round the room one after the other, with a little interval, and after conversing with the leading diplomatists, at length arrive where you are anxiously awaiting them. They then each, on your being presented to them separately, converse with you, on your name, &c., being announced, and I need not say have the tact to say something that is agreeable to yourself or your nation. The Czar spoke to me, among other things, of the Volunteers, admired the patriotic spirit they had displayed in enrolling themselves, and especially their motto of "Defence not defiance," and the Empress also very graciously addressed me subsequently. Her Majesty wore a low dress, with a long train of blue velvet, trimmed with Russian sable, and *such* diamonds and pearls. The Princess Dagmar has the same beautiful intelligent eyes as her sister, and I should have known her from the similitude in that feature alone, among all the ladies of the Court. She wore a white silk dress, covered with rare silver embroidery, and her ornaments were also diamonds and pearls. The Empress alone wore a train. After the presentations the Royal Family proceeded through the remaining rooms, where there were hundreds ranged on each side to receive them, bowing as they went, and receiving the respectful salutations of all.

The guard of honour was composed of Cossacks in one room, and of the Chevaliers of the Garde in another, and I was very much struck to-day, as I was some time ago, to see what a physiognomical resemblance there is among the men composing the regiments here. Passing by a barrack the other day, when the regiment of the Emperor Paul was just marching in, I stopped to observe them, and looking into their faces was intensely amused to see they were each " alike as two peas." *One* fellow with a celestial nose has a comical appearance, but fancy 500 passing before you, all with noses looking towards Heaven. After they had gone in, I had a good laugh, and turned to Ivan for the explanation, when he informed me that the men, bearing a resemblance to each other, are draughted into the same regiments, and that this one especially is a "celestial," the late Emperor Paul, who founded it, having been a celestial.

This brings me back into the streets again, and to the market here, where we were offered one night by the industrious vendors, anything, from a sucking pig to a defunct wolf, which we were invited to buy, and take home in our pockets. You need not go far here to find what you want, as the shops in the principal streets have everything displayed in tempting variety, and in the market streets, the outside of the shops, doors, balustrades, porticoes, &c., are covered with actual pictures of almost each article they sell. If you take your stand before a boot shop, and require a certain kind of boot or shoe (you need not enter if not inclined), until you have discovered they have the pattern you require, which you can do by examining all the pictures outside of every variety of boot and shoe they have within, but if you do enter, do not forget, however humble the dwelling, to take off your hat, first of all, out of respect to the tenant, and secondly, to the Shrine of the Virgin, or of the Saint which you always find placed in a corner of the room, whom the tenant particularly patronises, or who patronises him.

Wet nurses are a grand institution here, and when engaged in a lady's family, have a fine time of it, if one may judge by the magnificence of their appearance when they are out for an airing. They are arrayed in very pretty and very remarkable looking dresses, consisting of the Russian head ornament, which rises two or three inches above the forehead, and is covered with narrow silver braid, the gown and pelisse of bright blue or red cloth, ornamented also with broad silver braid, and the remainder of the costume quite in keeping with the above. When dressed in blue, it denotes that it is a little boy, who is the recipient of their bounty, and when in red, that it is a little girl. The Tartar hawkers are queer looking fellows; they sell all kinds of cotton goods in the streets, slung over their shoulders, and combining the gayest and most fantastic colours. Observe "Hisworshik," the Droshki man, bargaining for a sash he wants to present to his sweetheart for a New Year's gift. He is very cautious, and wets the sash with his finger, and rubs hard to ascertain whether the dye is hard and fast. We hear a tremendous hallooing in the distance, and presently comes past a fire brigade man, mounted on a galloping steed, clearing the way for the fire engine, which is following closely after him. (We might adopt the "avant courier" with advantage). There are a score of fire towers all over the town, on top of which are located watchers night and day, and by signals by day, and by lamps at night, give notice from each tower to he other when and where a fire takes place. (This system we might also adopt with still further advantage). The police are fine fellows here, and are admirably constituted. Some time ago a brave member of the force stopped a Troika, the three horses of which were running away and making for the crowded "Nevski," which, if it had reached, several persons must have been killed. The poor fellow was knocked down, but held on, though severely and mortally wounded. He was carried home, where he survived for some weeks, during which the Emperor visited him in person, gave him a distinguished order of merit, and assured him that his wife and children should have his especial care. This makes heroes of the men, as they know that their Czar's eye is, as it were, upon them, humble though they be. The Czar is the father of his people, and always addresses his soldiers as "my children," and the orphans of the military, as well as of others who have served the state, have establishments provided for their maintenance and education.

We were stopped on our walk this morning by a friend, who asked us if we had heard about the accident which had happened to Rushem-Pacha, the Turkish ambassador at this court, and he went on to relate that the ambassador had gone bear-hunting, and after having lodged a shot in the animal he attacked, the bear rushed upon him, and after discharging his revolver a second time without effect, the ambassador was obliged to have recourse to his poignard, and as the bear advanced, he drove this instrument down the animal's throat, but his own arm went with it, which Bruin terribly mangled before he could extricate it. At the same time the ambassador got his face much torn by one of the animal's paws, which, it is feared, will very much disfigure the ambassador. The Russian peasant who was with him took to his heels, but the bear was eventually shot by another attendant, and thus released the Pacha from any further trouble with the monstrous brute. Now, you must not think by this account that there is always as much danger in this sport as attended this particular instance, but the ambassador wanted all the glory by going comparatively alone, and the consequence was he got all the pain; they usually go out in large numbers, and the Emperor is very much addicted to it and is an excellent bear shot. And now I must confide a secret to you. A friend of mine who is in possession of a bear's lair has formed a party to hunt him, and I have gladly accepted an invitation to join them, as it is the thing to do in Russia, but I much fear that after this unfortunate accident, Louise will not exactly consent to it. However, "*Nous verrons.*" If I do go I will give you a full account of our adventure *if the bear will permit me.* Wolves form also very good sport. They are found in considerable numbers not far from St. Petersburg, as well as all over Russia. Another of my friend's expeditions, in which I am invited to take part, is a trip to Finland in a troika for the purpose of shooting the wolf. It seems that you take with you in your troika a live pig in a bag, and that when you get near the woods where you expect to find wolves you squeeze the pig, which makes him squeak, hearing which out come the wolves; the party then secure their opportunity by taking a shot at them. If one or more is killed you can't get at them, because if a male the rest of the pack remain to devour him, and if a female she is left where she falls, but war to the death is now waged between you and the wolves, their gallantry is called upon to revenge the premature death of one of their ladies, and you must keep on shooting a male, whom they will always stop to devour or get away from the scene of your exploits by galloping to more open country. In cases of difficulty, where the sportsmen are nervous and not good shots, or when ammunition is expended, in order to stop the wolves the pig is thrown overboard, and then if necessary one of the horses is killed and cast adrift, and sometimes even a second horse, leaving only one to pursue the journey, but all this is of course to give you time to get away, and to continually stop the wolves in their pursuit when they are infuriated and famished; because as long as you oblige the wolves with one of themselves, provided it is a male, or any other animal, yourself included, they remain to partake of your generous liberality.

But I don't think I have told you anything about the famous carriages of the country, the "troika" and the "chetverka." The first is a large car on a sleigh, drawn by three horses abreast, and holds four people inside, besides the driver, who stands in a sort of receptacle for his legs just inside the splash board. The centre horse has a grand and gorgeous yoke, which attaches him to the shafts, and the outside horses run along in traces. The harness is brilliant with silver plating, but, best of all, the pace they go at is most exhilarating, when you get into the open country, where the snow is in good condition for sledging, or, still better, on the ice on the river, or on the Gulf of Finland, and the driver exhorts his horses to increased action simply by his voice and the language he uses to them, which they seem perfectly to understand. Off they go at full gallop, which gives you the nearest idea to what must be the delightful sensation of flying, of which you can possibly conceive, and for miles and miles they will continue stretching away at a glorious pace, although, from the appearance of the animals, you would hardly consider them capable of it, but they are " very little fellows, and as hard as nails."

A "chetverka" is a four-horse carriage, but not used so much on a sleigh as on wheels in the summer. The four horses are harnesed abreast, but their position and action while in motion is most curious. The pair in the centre do most of the work and the outsiders represent effect, and in order to give you an idea of the appearance they present, first of all, imagine them to be all looking and standing straight to the front. Well, we will leave the centre horses in this position, and give our word of command to the near and off horses one after the other. Now for the horse on the near side. Attention! Left face! Left wheel! March! And just as he has complied with your instructions, and put out his left or near leg, to commence the march and wheel, halt him. And then you have him as he commences his gallop when started off. For the horse on the off side you reverse your word of command as regards his wheel, which must be right wheel, and you get both your horses facing outwards, and causing the four to present from the front the shape of an extended fan. Messrs. Passmore & Son, of Windsor, are building a new *char-à-banc* for Louise to drive her team of ponies in, but we are so delighted with the appearance of the chetverka, that she has asked me to break her little Exmoors into going four abreast, so that she may drive them occasionally in her *char-à-banc* in the Russian fashion.

We had a delightful drive in our troika one evening last week to the "Ice Hills," which afford much amusement here in winter. We had a few friends to dine with us, and after dinner our troikas were ordered round, and away we went up the Nevski, over the river Neva, with temporary lamp-posts erected on the ice, to direct the way, and arrived at full gallop at our destination. When we had mounted an immense flight of steps to get to the top of the ice hill, we reached a platform, from which you perceived a very precipitate descent of glittering ice, extending for some considerable distance. There you find the Russian guides, with their long flat pieces of board, covered with cloth, and fixed on to irons underneath exactly resembling skates. This is long enough for two people to sit upon, but very narrow, the guide behind to direct it in its flight over the ice, and you in front with nothing to hold on by. When thus arranged at the edge of the platform, your skating board is pushed forward, and in a moment you are off at the rate of at least sixty miles an hour, as hard as you can tear, down the ice hill. We hesitated some time before trusting ourselves to this amusement, but, summoning courage, I took the lead, and enjoyed it so much that I induced Louise and all the rest of the party to follow suit; and away we went, one after the other, helter skelter down the ice, almost taking your breath away before you eventually stop at the bottom, by a judiciously-placed layer of snow. Then up again, continually renewing the pleasurable excitement, until it was with difficulty we could make up our minds to enter the restaurant and take some tea, where we found music and dancing going on among the natives, which was another source of interest and gratification. At length we betook ourselves to our troikas about midnight, and, by the light of the moon, raced home over the snow and ice, each of us bribing our drivers to go as hard as they could tear along, and pass the others.

Just as I had got to this part of my letter, our door was opened, and Ivan brought in a large document, which, on opening, I found to contain invitations for Louise and myself from " Le Grand-Maitre des ceremonies," dating from " La Cour Imperiale," inviting us to be present at the palace on Thursday, the 6th of January (OS), to see the religious ceremony which takes place on the day of the Epiphany; so as, of course, we proposed to attend, I thought I would leave this letter open until to-day, and now we have been to the palace, and returned, I can give you a short account of it.

This day is the Russian 6th of January (the Epiphany), kept very sacredly by the Russian Church as the day on which our Saviour was baptised by St. John. Accordingly every year the Metropolitan, or Archbishop of St. Petersburg, accompanied by the Emperor, his sons, and all the male members of the Royal Family, form a grand religious procession, headed by representatives from all the Russian regiments with their colours, and proceed in state to a beautiful temple erected for the occasion immediately opposite the Palace, on the banks of the river Neva, to celebrate the baptismal ceremony. Such a sight of regal magnificence combining all the splendour of the grandest court in Europe, with a full display by a most pageantistic church, and realising to your mind a spirit of soul-felt devotion, I have never before witnessed. The long line of galleries, gorgeously decorated rooms, guards of soldiers from every regiment in St. Petersburg, hundreds of officers in full dress uniforms, with orders glittering with jewels, ambassadors from every court in Europe, and then the Emperor, with military music striking up by band after band as he passed along, created a sensation more easily felt than described. From the windows of the Palace we watched the ceremony. The Emperor, with all his court, the high priests of the Russian religion, countless thousands of his subjects, all stood bare-headed, with eight degrees of frost, while the archbishop offered up his prayer, and afterwards blessed the banners of the regiments of all Russia, by which he was surrounded. The religious ceremony terminated, the procession returned to the palace, passing through the rooms, the Emperor bowing to us all as we lined the way. To give you an idea of the liberality of the court as well as of its magnificence, there were upwards of 2,000 covers laid for a champagne *déjeuner à la fourchette* for those who were invited, and as we were in the circle of the diplomatic corps we had at our table the French, Austrian, and Portuguese ambassadors, Louise being seated next to General Le Flo, with whom I heard her discussing politics in connection with the future of the French, nation, but as the ambassador might object to his conversation being repeated I must refrain, although there was much in it that was deeply interesting.

I remain, MY DEAR JOHN,

Your affectionate Brother,

R. RICHARDSON-GARDNER.

Hôtel de Russie,
St. Petersburg,
10-22 *January*, 1872.

My dear John,

I have said in a previous letter that the Russians date their civilization from the reign of Peter the Great, and now I propose to take you through St. Petersburg, following those relics which appertain to his memory, from his cottage by the side of the Neva, built by himself, to his grave in the Cathedral of St. Peter and St. Paul.

Peter was a Romanoff, and was proclaimed Czar of all the Russias in 1689, being at that time only seventeen years of age. It is well known that, finding Russia much behind the rest of the world in mechanical and other arts, for which he personally had a great natural gift, he left his country for a time, much against the wishes of his family and friends, to make himself acquainted with the arts and inventions of other European nations, and used his tools as an ordinary workman in their principal dockyards. He visited England, and was well known in Gravesend, London, and other places on the banks of the Thames, and afterwards stayed some time in Holland, where he not only built, but sailed his own boat, which we have seen here, as well as specimens of his engraving, turning, and carpentering work. He rose at four in the morning, at six he was either in the Senate, or the Admiralty; he succeeded in forming and bringing into a high state of discipline a large army; he found Russia without a fishing smack, and bequeathed to her a navy, to which that of Sweden, long established and highly efficient, lowered her flag; he built St. Petersburg—turning a swamp into a great and magnificent city; he caused canals and other works of public utility to be constructed in various parts of the country; endowed colleges and universities; and generally promoted the advancement of his great empire.

And now we will go to his first work in Russia—the erection of his own hut, choosing a site from which he might superintend the mighty works he had carried out under his care. Here it is, for the most part just as he left it, with its three apartments—dining-room, reception-room, and bed-room—the first about ten feet square and the second about twelve feet square, the bed-room being smaller than either. The dining-room is now formed into a chapel or shrine, where hangs a picture of our Saviour, which always accompanied Peter in his travels; but the other rooms are unaltered. One arm-chair of his own make stands in a corner. The whole cottage is now enclosed for preservation by an exterior shell, leaving passage room between. His next thought, after his home, was his church, and he therefore had a small church of wood erected, which was the original cathedral, and here it stands in its primitive form, and in which there is service at this present day. When the building of St. Petersburg had progressed, it became necessary for Peter to have a larger domicile than the cottage, as he had no convenience even to receive people for the transaction of business, so he selected a large piece of ground, and planted the present Summer Garden, and in one corner of it had a house built, which is about the size of a very small French château, and in which also a few articles of furniture used by Peter are carefully preserved.

We will now go to the Museum of Imperial Carriages and look round us for something commemorative of Peter. What do we see first? On the top of the staircase is the skeleton of a horse, not Peter's, but that of the late Emperor Nicholas, whose favourite charger he was. An inscription attached to the skeleton states that the horse was twenty-five years old when he died, and had been ridden by the Emperor for many years. Inside this gallery we find the Imperial Coronation and other gala carriages, all of the most costly description, with ornamented panels containing exquisite pictures by Boucher, Gravelot, and other eminent artists. These carriages are only used at the coronation of the Emperors or Empresses at Moscow, to which place they are carefully transported. It is interesting to look at the carriages, which have been used by a line of sovereigns, while on their way to be crowned autocrats of dominions extending over one-half of Europe and nearly one-half of Asia. At last we come to the greatest curiosity in the gallery, a covered sledge made by Peter entirely with his own hands. It is a small, close carriage, fitted as a sledge, with broad, strong slides; the windows are made of isinglass, and it is lined with green baize. Behind there is a small trunk, which contained the clothes and provisions of the great Czar when he travelled. An extra fee to the custodian gained us permission to enter this remarkable carriage, built by an Emperor, and in which he is said to have traversed his dominions.

The Imperial library contains a room of engravings dedicated to Peter the Great's time, among which are many of his own likenesses, but the most amusing one of all is on a common, ordinary, swing sign board, such as they used at taverns and hostelries in times past, and which may still be seen swinging in English country districts. One Edward Wilde kept a tavern at Gravesend, which was frequented by the Czar, and the said Edward Wilde, seeing the advantage such a customer gave him, and being a bit of an artist, slyly painted the portrait of Peter and hung it up outside his house, with the inscription of "The Czar of Muscovy" on the top, and his own name of Edward Wilde, as landlord, at the bottom. Peter was good natured enough to allow it to remain, and report says Edward Wilde drove a good trade, people coming from miles round to see the wonderful "Czar of Muscovy" without, and within. We were much interested in examining the rare MSS. and missals in this famous collection, they bore picture engravings of almost every celebrated person that has lived in Europe, whatever has been his calling, and underneath one or more letters, or at least autographs of each. Great Britain is partly represented by letters or autographs of Henry VII., Henry VIII., Elizabeth, James I., Charles I., and Queen Henrietta, Robert Devereux Earl of Essex, &c., but probably the most interesting of all are several letters of Mary Queen of Scots, addressed by her to different people of her time, as well as a missal, or diary, where you may read the passing thoughts of her mind during her great trouble. Near the beginning is written, "*Ce livre est a moi Marie Reine*, 1553." Letters from English statesmen, men of letters, and anyone celebrated in any way, are here placed under glass cases, and beautifully arranged, so that you can easily and comfortably read them. I copied one from Richard Cobden, and here it is:—

"Mr. Cobden presents his compliments to Messrs. Pritt, Venables, and Co., and begs to say that with his strong opinions against any further railways being authorised at present he will not be justified in having his name on the Barnsley Bill."

We will now go to the Hermitage, where I won't detain you with any lengthened description of its splendid collection of pictures, more than to say that it contains a rare selection, numbering 1635, including the Italian, Spanish, Flemish, Dutch, German, French, Russian, and English schools, each artistically classed; besides an extensive numismatic collection, as one also of rare gems, and lastly, Peter the Great's gallery, which is replete with his personal effects and relics, among which are the turning lathes, and instruments for carving with which the Monarch worked; his telescopes, mathematical instruments, books, and walking sticks, are all objects of great curiosity. A rod giving his height, shows him to have been of the gigantic stature of seven feet. Here is a dress worn by him, and embroidered by his wife Catherine the First, for the ceremony of her coronation, and is appropriately placed in the centre of this interesting workshop and museum. And now we approach the last resting place of this marvellous man, near which in an outside building exists, quite as complete as he left it, the boat he built with his own hands, and on the stern of which he carved a picture of its launch, himself standing by, and the priest blessing it as it lay on the water. In the cathedral of St. Peter and St. Paul, lies buried Peter the Great, and all the sovereigns of Russia since the foundation of St. Petersburg, excepting only Peter II. who died and was interred at Moscow. The bodies are deposited under the floor of the church, the marble

tombs above only marking the sites of the graves. The following are the names of some of those members of the Romanoff Royal family who are here interred:—
Peter the Great, and Empress Catherine the First, his wife. Empress Elisabeth, daughter of Peter the Great. Empress Anne, niece of Peter the Great. Emperor Peter the Third, nephew of Peter the Great. Empress Catherine the Second. Emperor Alexander the First, and Empress Elisabeth, his wife. Emperor Paul, and Empress Mary, his wife. Emperor Nicholas, and Empress Alexandra, his wife. Grand Duke Constantine, brother to Emperor Nicholas. A baby of the present Crown Prince. A daughter of the present Emperor. The Czarewitch (Grand Duke Nicholas), eldest son of the present Emperor.

The late Czarewitch, the eldest son of the present Emperor Alexander, you will remember, died at Nice, and round his tomb and those of the more recently deceased, exotic and other plants are grouped. He was the pride and hope of his house, and beloved by the Russian people. I cannot do better than to give you in conclusion of this part of my letter a very graphic description from *Free Russia* :—" One dark December day, near dusk, two Englishmen hail a boat on the Neva brink, and push out rapidly through the bars of ice towards that grim fortress of St. Peter and St. Paul, in which lie buried, under marble slab and golden cross, the Emperors and Empresses (with one exception) since the reign of Peter the Great. As they are pushing onward they observe the watermen drop their oars and doff their caps, and looking round, they see the imperial barge, propelled by twenty rowers, athwart their stern. The Emperor Alexander sits in that barge alone, an officer is standing by his side, and the helmsman directs the rowers how to pull. Saluting as he glides past their boat, the Emperor jumps to land, and muffling his loose great coat about his neck, steps hastily along the planks, and up the roadway leading to the church. No one goes with him. The six or eight idlers who he meets on the road just touch their hats, and stand aside to let him pass. Trying the front door of the sombre church, he finds it locked, and striding off quickly to a second door, he sees a man in plain clothes, and beckons to him. The door is quickly opened, and the lord of seventy millions of subjects walks into the church that is to be his final home. The English visitors are near. 'Wait for an instant,' says the man in plain clothes, 'the Emperor is within;' but adds, 'You can step into the porch, His Majesty will not keep you long.' The porch is parted from the church by glass doors only, and the English visitors look down upon the scene within. Long aisles and columns stretch and rise before them; flags and trophies, won in a hundred battles, fought against the Swede and Frank, the Perse and Turk, adorn the walls; and here and there a silver lamp burns fitfully in front of a pictured Saint. Between the columns stand, in white sepulchral rows, the Imperial tombs, a weird and ghostly vista, gleaming in this red and sombre light, alone. The Emperor passes from slab to slab; now pausing for an instant, as if conning an inscription on the stone; now crossing the nave absorbed and bent; here hidden for a moment in the gloom; then moving furtively along the aisle. The dead are all around him; Peter, Catherine, Paul; fierce warriors; tender women; innocent babes; and overhead the dust and glory of a hundred wars. What brings him hither in this wintry dusk? He stops and

and kneels at the foot of his mother's tomb! Once more he pauses, kneels, kneels a long time, as if in prayer; then, rising, kisses the golden cross. That slab is the tomb of his eldest son! A moment later he is gone."

And now, my dear John, to what ordinary subject can I descend? How am I to glide from the grave to the gay? Theatres? No; too sudden. The ball at the Palace on Monday last? Worse still. I will keep that to finish with. I have it; something I will tell you about some Laplanders, or more properly Samoyeds, who have just arrived, and are encamped on the river. We went down to pay them a visit, and entered one of their shanties, where a small family of two mothers, one father, and a heap of children were congregated, feeding on raw fish, and picking the bones of a deceased reindeer. They were a curious lot. What a world this is! as a friend of mine used constantly to remark. Here was this Samoyed family before us, where we were quite safe from their rapacious eyes and stomachs; but if they had happened to have got one of us alone in their own particular country, they might be picking our bones instead of those of the reindeer; because this same race are reputed to be cannibals, when they are hard up for food, which is their normal state. These Samoyeds are nomadic, cowering through the winter months in shanties, sprawling through the summer months in tents, their shanty is a pyramid with a roll of reindeer skins, drawn slackly round a series of poles, and an opening at the top to let out the smoke. The women, looking anything but lovely in their sealskin tights and reindeer smocks, are infamous for magic and second sight. In every district of the north a female Samoyed is feared as a witch, an enchantress, who keeps a devil by her side, bound to obey her will. Over the greater part of their country the snow never melts, but in June the slopes of a few favoured valleys grow green with reindeer moss. On this the reindeer feed, and on these, when he can get them, and on raw fish, the wild men of the country live. Samoyed means cannibal,—man eater;—they use no fire in cooking food, and hence, probably, the horrible fame they have acquired, which, after all, like many other ill used people, they may not deserve; but I would rather not try. They are evidently brought to St. Petersburg by an enterprising *entrepreneur* who gathers unto himself many copecks for the exhibition; and one of the amusements we entered into for a consideration was a drive in the reindeer sleigh; quite in the "Chetvertka" style, four reindeer abreast, down the Neva and back, all for the small charge of ten copecks each.

Well now, I said I would finish with the ball, and as ladies can describe such festivities with a great deal more grace than gentlemen, I have, with Louise's permission, extracted from a letter she has just written a friend, her pretty account of it:—

"The ball is already an event of the past, inasmuch as it came off on Monday night, and how I am to describe it is a mystery to me, as no language I can use can give you the faintest idea of the reality. If you have read the 'Arabian Nights,' you will remember the story of Aladdin's wonderful fairy palace. Try and imagine a suite of some nine or ten large galleried rooms, supported by white marble pillars, richly decorated ceilings, white and gold, adorned also with much looking-glass, opening each out of the other, lighted not only by the wax candles in the massive crystal chandeliers, but by, I may literally say, myriads of candles placed in circles around each column from base to pinnacle, and also surrounding the galleries and windows like an illumination. Add to this, beautiful exotics, from floor to roof, in the four corners of each room, with two palm trees in the centre of the principal ball-room, bands of military music striking up in succession, sixteen hundred of the *haute noblesse* of the Empire, in all the variety of ball attire and military full dress, and you may, perhaps, in some degree imagine the scene which our eyes and senses took in upon our first arrival at the Winter Palace, at half-past nine o'clock, on Monday evening. Of course, Royalty had not yet entered, as all the guests must be in waiting to receive them, and a right Royal party they did look when, a few minutes later, there was a commotion among the masters of the ceremonies, and a 'hush' from all, and then the Emperor, leading the Empress, the Crown Prince, with his wife, the Princess Dagmar (our Princess of Wales' sister), the grand Duchess Mary (the Emperor's only daughter), with the other princes, and all the other members of the court enter, and after having been received by deep obeisances from all, the ball commences by the Crown Prince leading off the Empress, and the Emperor the Crown Princess; but here I must say one word relative to the Empress's diamonds. The tunic of her dress was embroidered with the Imperial bee in diamonds; the under skirt embroidered with bouquets of raised flowers, the petals of each flower diamonds; a fringe of diamonds surrounding the low body of her dress, a bouquet of diamonds forming the stomacher; and as for the diamond pendants to her necklace, and the diamond tiara on her head, I can give you no idea of their costliness. But now the first dance is over; the ladies to be presented to the Empress are conducted to an adjoining room, where they are placed in a circle, and the Empress, with one gentleman in attendance to announce our names to her, enters, and on being presented in her turn she finds something graceful and amiable to say to each, as she slowly walks round the expectant circle. This ceremony over, we all return to the ball-room, and dancing continues until midnight, the Princesses entering into the spirit of it with evident enjoyment, meanwhile the Emperor and Empress talking, and making, in course of time, the whole tour of the numerous rooms. The whole evening refreshments of every variety are to be procured at a buffet, extending along a gallery, which runs parallel to the three largest ball-rooms. Here heaps of gold plate are piled up in pyramids at intervals, the whole length of the gallery; and now to supper. A hot one, and everyone seated. The tables are so sumptuously decorated with gold and silver plate, the only thing I can think of to compare it to, would be an exhibition of all the race cups of the last fifty years. There are three supper rooms, but as we are "distinguished strangers," we sup with the diplomatic corps, at a table adjoining the Emperor's, which is slightly raised upon a däis. After supper, which lasts nearly an hour, the Royal party retire, and we leave soon after, being most delighted, and wonderfully impressed by the magnificence of the Royal entertainment we have attended. I feel I have told my story but ill, but it is impossible to give in words any description, or any idea of the great luxury at this court, which combines Oriental and Asiatic splendour with European taste and civilisation. Everyone is equally impressed by it, therefore, you must not think it any excited enthusiasm on my part, as the Greek minister said to me, 'It is magnificent,' and I repeat ' magnificent ; ' and all I can say is that it is magnificent, as there is no other word to convey my feelings, and so I must conclude by repeating it, 'magnificent.' "

I remain, MY DEAR JOHN,

Your affectionate Brother,

R. RICHARDSON-GARDNER.

HÔTEL DUSAUX,

Moscow,

18-30 *January*, 1872.

MY DEAR JOHN,

Moscow! holy Moscow; the ancient capital of Muscovy, the idol of every Russian's heart, whose shrines are to him the holiest in the empire, hallowed by centuries of grand historical events. What associations do not arise at the name? Moscow! the beautiful; Moscow! the unfortunate. What vicissitudes of good and evil fortune has this city not passed through? Four times nearly consumed by fire—in 1536, by accident; in 1572, by the Tartars, when over 100,000 persons perished in the flames, or by the sword; in 1611, by the Poles, who destroyed by fire a great portion of the city; and lastly, in 1812, when the Muscovites gave up their ancient, holy, and beautiful city to the devouring element, the grandest sacrifice ever made to national feeling. The plague of 1771 diminished the population by several thousands, from which it has never recovered, and the history of its battles and its sieges would alone fill many volumes. Take for instance one of the entrance gates to the Kremlin, say the Nikolsky gate, under whose arches the troops of Tokhtamysh, of Sigismund III. and of Napoleon, have all marched within four centuries. In 1408, it witnessed the siege of Moscow, by Edigei; in 1551, the invasion by the Crim Tartars; and in

1611–12, the battles between the Poles and the Russians for the possession of holy Moscow; and in 1812, Napoleon passed through it when it was partly destroyed by his orders, but subsequently restored, by order of the Emperor Alexander I. of Russia.

But in this letter it is not my intention to revert to much of its ancient history, only so far as it is connected with its modern aspect. And now let me place myself on top of the tower of Ivan Veliki, and take a bird's-eye view of the town, and dot down what appearance it presents. In my various wanderings, I have travelled through Asia Minor, and the North of Africa, and I have floated on the Golden Horn, with Constantinople within my view, but I have never yet seen any town or city which presented a *coup d'œil*, so truly Oriental or Asiatic as Muscovy's honoured capital, the view from the summit of this tower being certainly one of the most striking and unique in Europe. I have immediately under and about me the most ancient and most historical part of Moscow, and four of probably the most interesting buildings in the world, all within a stone's throw of each other. First, the Kremlin, for centuries the palace of the ancient Tsars of Muscovy, which has been the happy home of many, but also the scene of the most deplorable and wicked acts of which history is cognizant. Second, the Blagoveschenski Sobor, or Cathedral of the Annunciation, where the Tsars were baptized and married. Third, the Uspenski Sobor, or Cathedral of the Assumption, where the Tsars were, and are still crowned. Fourth, the Arkhangelski Sobor, or Cathedral of the Archangel Michael, where the ancient Tsars were buried, the present dynasty finding their last resting place as I have in a former letter informed you, in the cathedral of St. Peter and St. Paul, at St. Petersburg. Thus truly you may pass from the " cradle to the grave," for here lie buried Emperors of such good repute that they have been immortalised by their subjects as Saints, with others whose characters are too truly depicted by the cognomen they bore, and such a one was John the Terrible. All these buildings are in the Oriental style of architecture, with scores of domes and gilded minarets sparkling in the mid-day sun. The late Emperor Nicholas added a large and handsome *façade* to the old palace, much extending its interior accommodation for modern requirements. The Kremlin Palace, with its cathedrals. monasteries, and other buildings, is enclosed within battlements of solid masonry, and pierced by five gates, the principal of which is the Spaski, or Redeemer gate, which is the " Porta Sacra " and " Porta Triumphalis " of Moscow. Over it is a picture of the Redeemer, held in high veneration by the orthodox. An omission to uncover the head while passing under this gate was anciently punishable, and the traveller should not fail to pay the respect to old traditions here exacted, since the Emperor himself conforms to the custom. Criminals executed in front of this gate offered their last prayers on earth to this image of the Redeemer. Beyond we see a city, whose circumference is about twenty English miles, built totally irrespective of form, but presenting to the eye a pleasing negligence and picturesque irregularity ; houses large and small, public buildings, churches, and other edifices, are mingled confusedly together, and the streets undulate continually, and thus offer from time to time points of view, whence the eye is able to range over the vast area of housetops, trees, and gilded and coloured domes. The profusion of churches (370 in number) is a characteristic feature of the city. The other objects which most attract the observer, are the Foundling Hospital, the Treasury, the Arsenal, the Bazaar, the University, the Museum, the great Riding School, the Strastny, the Donskoé, the Simonoff, and Novopaski Monasteries, and the Novo-Devichi Convent, the Petrofski Park and Palace, and the Hermitage and Zoological Gardens.

And now I descend from the Ivan Veliki tower, and enter the ancient part of the Kremlin Palace by the red steps, which are now only used on important occasions, such as when the Emperor goes to the Cathedral of the Assumption. Now, here is a trifle of history for you to ruminate over. "From the top of these stairs the Tsars of old allowed the populace to see the light of their eyes; here John the Terrible gazed at the comet that seemed to foretell his speedy end; and it was here also that he committed the inhuman act of transfixing with his pointed staff the foot of the trusty messenger and friend of Prince Kurbski, a valiant leader of his armies, who, in the apprehension of unmerited punishment and death, fled to the Polish camp at Wolmar, whence he wrote to the Tsar, setting forth the crimes and atrocities of his reign; the tyrant rested on his staff while the letter was read by his comrades, the messenger meanwhile standing motionless and silent. From the red staircase the mangled body of the false Demetrius was thrown down in the court below by the infuriated people of Moscow, in 1606, and it was from the same steps that the rebel Streltsi, in 1682, tore the obnoxious Boyar Matveyeff, and cut him to pieces before the eyes of the terrified mother of Peter the Great, and numerous other noblemen and adherents of the court. By these steps, also, Napoleon, followed by his marshals, ascended to take possession of the Palace of the Kremlin." However, these steps lead to a gold court, an audience chamber, and banquetting-room, and also to the Hall of St. Vladimir, to which the Tsars proceed immediately after their coronation, and take their seats upon the throne for the first time, adorned with all the Imperial insignia, and afterwards dine amidst their nobles, crowned heads being alone seated at the same table. We now come to a very interesting part of the palace, the Terem, anciently devoted to the Tsarevna and her children. The rooms contain many objects of great curiosity, among which are the bed of Alexis, father of Peter the Great, just as he left it when carried to his grave; seals of many of the sovereigns, especially a gold seal of John the Terrible, which has sealed the doom of thousands, and which is almost painful to behold from its unhappy associations. Then more rooms, such as the Hall of the Patriarchs, &c., too numerous to particularise, on to the modern part of the palace, built by Nicholas. There we have on the ground floor all the private apartments of the Emperor and Empress, and the upper floor, containing the State apartments, which are as grand and as gorgeous as an autocratic emperor like Nicholas, with untold means at his command, could make them. There are several large halls, among which are the hall of St. Andrew and the hall of St. George, the latter 200 feet long, 68 feet broad, and 58 feet high, where the names of each individual decorated with this order since its foundation is to be found inscribed upon the walls in letters of gold; the furniture is black and orange—the colours of the order. There is also a picture gallery, containing, among others, some fine pictures brought here from the Royal Castle at Warsaw, upon seeing which Louise pitied the poor Poles, and, addressing herself to Ivan, lamented that Russia should so have despoiled Poland, upon which Ivan asked us where was the Kertch collection? and entertained us by the following narrative:—He said " when he was at the American Embassy at St. Petersburg, as chasseur, it became his duty to attend Governor Seymour, the American Minister, to Kertch, after the Crimean War as interpreter; and when there Governor Seymour, without giving his name, visited the museum, and inquired of the Russian director of the museum what had become of certain objects of interest which he had expected to find there? upon which the Russian director asked Ivan confidentially whether the gentleman was an Englishman, and on hearing from Ivan that he was an American, the Russian director broke out into great lamentation and anger, and said that the English had despoiled his museum to enrich their own at home." *Aliena nobis nostra plus aliis placent.*

And now we enter the treasury, which is the depository of venerated historical objects and of treasures hereditary in the reigning house, as the immense riches amassed here, consisting of gold and silver plate, of antique pattern and shape, precious stones of the rarest quality and value, and costly manufactures of different kinds, take hours to see. I cannot attempt to give you any definite idea of them in detail, but will only mention one or two objects which are more striking because of their historical associations. Fowling pieces, inscribed as having been presented in 1614 to the Tsar Michael (the first Romanoff) by Favian Smith, an Englishman; the standard of John the Terrible, planted at Kazan in 1552 on conquering that Province, as well as the pointed spear stick, which he did not hesitate to drive into the foot of anyone who offended him; also the Order of the Garter and the patent for it, sent by our Queen Elizabeth to this horrible ruffian. The sword and spurs of Charles XII. of Sweden, which he wore at the battle of Poltava; coronation chairs of the Empress Elizabeth, Paul I., Alexander II., and several others bearing their respective ciphers; the throne of Poland, removed from Warsaw and used by Nicholas as King of that conquered country; the insignia of Alexis, of Peter the Great, and his brother John. An ivory throne, date 1472 (just four hundred years old), which the present Emperor Alexander used at his coronation. Near it a throne used by Alexis, studded with 876 diamonds and 1223 rubies, besides turquoise and pearls. An orb of great historical importance, sent by the Greek Emperors Basilius and Constantine to a Prince of Russia; it is most splendidly studded with 58 diamonds, 89 rubies, 23 sapphires, 50 emeralds, and 37 pearls, all of immense size and lustre. Next come different objects, viz., the *actual* coronation robes worn by several of the Tsars and their Empresses, military uniforms, and the ordinary jack boots of Peter the Great, Peter the Second, and Paul. Then come the crowns of the different monarchs, and among them we find those of Poland, Kazan, and other conquered kingdoms, and if our Government pusillanimously give way, as they have lately done on the Black Sea Treaty question ("Ex uno disce omnes"), the Russians will soon add the crowns from Constantinople, in the southeast of Europe, and from Bokhara, in the north-west of India, to their already rather extensive collection. Beds of different monarchs are also exhibited here, and two camp bedsteads which belonged to Napoleon, one of which was used by him on the night of the battle of Berezina, when they were taken by the Russians.

And now, my dear John, as I fear I shall weary you with descriptions, I will take you to a " Traktir," where I have no doubt you would like to have joined us in discussing a Russian dinner, accompanied by Russian wines, in a Russian Restaurant. We ordered our dinner in the morning, and on arriving at the appointed hour of seven o'clock, found all ready. I don't know whether I have previously mentioned to you that Colonel Money went off to Southern Russia soon after our arrival at St. Petersburg, and Colonel Isenbeck (the Russian), by rail to Nijni-Novgorod, and after that by sleigh for forty days and nights to the " Amoor " river to his duty there (that's a nice journey in the dead of winter), but we were joined by an English friend on our visit to Moscow, the pleasure of whose company we had at dinner. For the amusement of the ladies I will describe him as being twenty-eight years of age, fair complexion, tall and elegant in figure, expressive eyes, and altogether very good looking. The diner-à-la-Russe commences with the " Zakuska." It consists of various relishes, such as fresh caviar, raw herring, smoked salmon, " Balyk " (sturgeon dried in the sun), raw smoked goose, radishes, cheese, butter, and other comestibles; these need not be specified in your menu, the word " Zakuska " comprehending everything of the kind in season. A liqueur glass of Kümmel (Alasch), flavoured with carraway seeds, or of Listofka, flavoured with the young leaves of the black currant, is taken after the Zakuska, which is laid out on a separate table, and is partaken of, all standing round. We then take our seats at the regular dinner table, and here is our menu:—

GREAT MOSCOW TRAKTIR.

Menu, 14th *Jan.*, o.s., 1872.

SOUP.
(*A small portion of each*).
Ukhà.
Rastigai.
Solianka.

FISH.
Sturgeon.
Rastikai.

Pojarskié Rotlety.

Utka y-Riabchiky.

Kuriefskaya Kata.

Nesselidde.

WINES
(*From the Crimea*).
Donskoé Champanskoé.
Kraonaju Kirmsk.
Kapétinskoé.

Now there's a puzzle for you, but take my word for it, it was all good and well-served by the most civil of waiters, attired only in bright-coloured silk shirts, with clean white trousers. After dinner we went to another "Traktir" to partake of the celebrated yellow Caravan tea, "Joltoi Chai," which comes overland from China, and is served in tumblers with a slice of lemon and sugar. Try a cup of tea in that fashion, and tell me when you write how you like it, only you may not have the "Joltoi Chai," which is important. You must know in all the tea-drinking rooms there is a large barrel organ, worked by machinery, which plays the most select and fashionable music from the most popular operas; and so we drank our tea to the strains of this instrument, the polite attendant bringing us a list of the pieces for Louise to make her selection. The natives sweeten their tea with a piece of sugar kept in the mouth; perhaps that would not exactly suit you, so I shall not recommend it.

But I have not yet told you how we got to Moscow, which was, of course, by train, leaving St. Petersburg at seven o'clock in the evening, and arriving here at eleven o'clock next morning (only sixteen hours), which we think a bagatelle now. There are carriages divided into half-compartments, and we took one for sixty roubles (about eight guineas), and made ourselves quite comfortable. I seem destined to be in the company of amusing stove-keepers, as our present one (a good-looking young man this time, of about thirty-five years of age), very soon began to speak a few English words, and informed me that he was married to an "Eengleesh vooman, a veery nice vooman," and *she* spoke a "leetle Ruski," and *he* spoke a "leetle Eengleesh," but neither of them spoke a word of each other's language when they married. What ceremony they went through, if any, I could not fathom, nor how they managed to make known "their loves," but probably it was through the medium of their eyes, as he had a brilliant pair of light blue. The poor fellow kept the stoves all right, and was duly rewarded with copecks at the end of our journey. When we arrived at our hotel we were surprised to find that the landlord had prepared a suite consisting of six rooms for us, which he said was in accordance with our telegram, so we requested to see it, and here it is as delivered:—" Hotel Dusaux, Moscow. Prepare sitting-wom and bedrom 4 gentleman and lady, leaving here seven glok hafn thes evening.—Gardner, St. Petersburg."—It appears that the clerk who sent it must have imagined himself very clever, and turned my " for," which he imagined to be " four," into the figure 4, and so prepared for us an immense reception and a disappointment to our host. I could not make out how our rooms were heated, as I examined all round our " sitting-wom," and could find no trace of hot-air pipe or stove; but on retiring to my little bed I soon jumped out, as I touched something awfully hot with my feet, and on lighting the candle again I found the stove, which was lighted from the outside passage, ran along level with the wall, and, although not easily noticeable, was sensibly felt. I managed to intercept the heat with a non-conductor, and only left enough to be comfortable, and I never slept better in my life; in fact, I began to like it, which accounts for ladies taking to " hot bottles."

The next evening we had an adventure, a short narrative of which I sent to *The Times*, and headed it "Moscow—A warning," in which I said " That as the Moscow Exhibition is in the course of erection, and doubtless there would be several of our countrymen here in the autumn months, I considered it my duty to send them a warning not to go beyond the precincts of the city either on foot or in a public vehicle, unless properly accompanied," but as I don't know whether *The Times* has or will publish my letter, I send you a short account of what occurred.

Ivan, our dragoman, suggested that we should go to evening service in the church of the Strastny Convent, where all the prayers and ceremonies are performed by the nuns, to which we readily assented. Issuing forth, therefore, from our hotel, Ivan hails " Hisvorshik," and directs the driver to take us to the convent; Ivan intending to follow us closely in another sleigh, as they only accommodate two. The convent is within the city, although we were unaware of its *locale*, and therefore, when the driver took us out of the city, through the St. Petersburg gate, we thought it was all right, as many of the monastic establishments are some way beyond the town. However, I looked behind for Ivan two or three times, and began to wonder why he had not kept up with us, when at last I saw him galloping after us at a furious rate, and on overtaking our sleigh, he jumped out, caught hold of our man's reins, and a serious row commenced, Ivan charging our driver with not obeying his instructions, and attempting to take us, knowing us to be foreigners, out to a village called Sisvjatsky, a place of evil notoriety, about a mile in the suburbs, for the purpose of getting us robbed by his accomplices there. It seems our driver didn't know that Ivan intended to follow us, so thought he could take us with impunity where he pleased, and the misfortune of the horse in Ivan's sleigh falling, facilitated his designs, so that Ivan was delayed until he could procure another sleigh. He then drove to the convent, and finding we were not there, and had been seen going down another road, his suspicions were awakened, and he drove at a gallop after us, overtaking us when we were within a quarter of a mile of what appears to be about the worst place near Moscow, inhabited by a lawless lot of ruffians.

I could hardly credit Ivan's suspicions until we returned to our hotel, when they were entirely confirmed by Russians and others connected with the place, who said that it was not an unusual occurrence for foreigners, and even Russians (when inebriated) to be taken there, hustled by these roughs, robbed of their furs and valuables, and then let loose to find their way back to Moscow as best they could.

We, however, got back to the convent in time for the conclusion of the service, and the sweet silvery voices of the nuns, as they chanted the responses, soon made us forget all about the Sisvjatsky villagers, and our narrow escape from their polite attentions.

I remain, MY DEAR JOHN,

Your affectionate brother,

R. RICHARDSON-GARDNER.

HÔTEL DUSAUX,
Moscow,
20th Jan.—(1st Feb., 1872.)

MY DEAR JOHN,

Foundling Hospitals! Now, I don't intend to enter upon the question as to whether such institutions tend to recognise and increase immorality, but simply to give you a short account of a most interesting visit which we have to-day paid to the largest hospital of the kind in existence, viz., that at Moscow. We had previously gone through the Foundling at St. Petersburg, which is a branch of the institution here, and we were so interested with the *child* that we determined to visit its *parent*.

The Foundling Hospital at Moscow was opened in 1763 by Empress Catherine II., and in the year of grace 1871, about 12,000 children were received at its doors, not, as at some other institutions, in a secret manner, but openly, and taken either by the mother or some friend into an entrance room set apart for that purpose. There the infant is at once received without any further question being asked than, has the child been baptised! and if so, by what name? The child is then registered in the books of the institution, and a number is assigned to it, which is henceforward worn around its neck, and figures on its cot, while a receipt showing the same number, is handed to the bearer of the child, in order to enable her to visit, or even claim it, at any future period up to the age of ten years, in which case all its expenses have to be paid. The infant is then passed into another room, where, after being undressed washed, and weighed, it is swaddled in the clothes of the hospital and handed to its future foster parent, she being the woman who happens at the moment to stand at the head of the list amongst a number who are always waiting in attendance. These women, who are generally peasants from the country, have frequently, it is believed, themselves been the depositors of their own children at the hospital, either personally or by means of a friend, a few hours previously; but be that as it may, the nurses who support the children's existence are provided with good fare at the institution, and are paid about 8d. a day, which I fear is an attraction many of the peasant women seek, at the expense of their own offspring, who are left in their villages, to be brought up by hand. We saw two infants arrive while we were in the room where they are received, and go through the operation of being washed and weighed, the poor little things were respectively twenty-four and thirty hours old, and looked in very good condition, being, we were informed, about the average weight. One was a boy, and the other a girl, the boy having a blue ribbon attached to his cap, and the girl a red, which is the distinction of the sexes right through the institution. In the first ward there were about thirty little ones, all recent arrivals, with red and blue ribbons, and ensconced in such neat clean little cribs, with a foster mother to each, rocking it in its cradle, or imparting to it its nourishment, and following on, there were wards seemingly without end, all full of children in cradles, and nurses attending them, the latter all being clad in a hospital uniform of brown holland, with clean white caps, plaited frills with narrow dark blue ribbon, all well behaved, who respectfully bowed as our party passed. The children are all vaccinated at three weeks old, from calves kept for the purpose on the establishment, and passed on from ward to ward, until they are about six or eight weeks old, when, if they are strong and healthy, they are sent together with their nurses to the villages to which the latter belong, where the nurses receive about 4s. 6d. a month for the maintenance of their charges, under the supervision of the government doctor of the district. I am strongly of opinion that many mothers bring their legitimate children up from the country, get them in at one door, and enter themselves at another as nurses; get appointed to be foster mothers to their own children, and so get paid for nursing them eventually at their own domestic hearths. Well, suppose they do, the humbler classes are very poor in Russia, and live a very hard life, and if they procure this small assistance from the Government, the rich don't feel it, and the poor much need it, and Russia has not yet arrived at those refined principles of social science which would permit a child to starve if the parent was too poor to keep it alive. Poor little Atoms! In one ward there was a steam apparatus, for hatching the prematures into vitality; there were four such little weeny things undergoing the process, the whole four not weighing much more than a full grown child, the weight of each being registered on the wall over its head. The doctor who accompanied us said they were very successful with them, if they only lived long enough to get them under or rather over steam. Next to the prematures there were three babies (I was going to say twins, but I think they are called triplets), two girls and a boy, all together in one cradle, born of one mother, and brought in on Christmas Eve;

weight of the three on arrival 17¼lbs.; they were all mercifully asleep, so we had a quiet look at them, and wondered where and who their mother could be.

By-the-bye, we were astonished at the quietude of the place, with seven to eight hundred babies under one roof, and so little crying, which we were assured was in consequence of the great care and attention paid to them, and which we could not fail to perceive, as nothing which good domestic management can suggest, or medical art approve, has been omitted. The boys, when they grow up, generally become agricultural labourers. Some of the more intelligent are brought up at the Industrial Schools at Moscow and St. Petersburg, where they are taught various trades, and may also become hospital dressers at the School of Surgery. Some of the girls are taken back to the institution, and trained as nurses, and even sometimes as midwives, for which a special school is attached. In taking leave, I came to the conclusion that there is a political foundation for keeping up these large foundling hospitals beyond the feeling of philanthrophy or humanitarianism, which is, that Russia has a larger tract of country than it can conveniently populate, and population being essential to the progress and advancement of the Russian empire, the state protects the lives of its infantile subjects, legitimate or illegitimate.

And now we find our pair horse sleigh ready waiting at the door to take us into the country to visit what are popularly called the "Sparrow hills," a range forming a semi-circle round Moscow, about six miles distant from the city. This drive is particularly interesting, both as affording a fine view of Moscow, and as being the ground where Napoleon obtained his first glance of it, and being also the same route by which his army entered the city. On our way we stopped at the Novo-Devitche Convent, and had the pleasure of seeing all the nuns in the Refectory enjoying their mid-day meal. This was only allowed as Louise was of our party, otherwise no gentlmen are admitted alone; but they need not have been alarmed, as I thought they were all extremely plain and uninteresting, although Reginald A—— said he caught a sly glimpse of a very pretty face under the black fantastic and most unbecoming hood. Our sleigh followed us from the convent to the hills, when we had the full enjoyment of a walk over the hard crisp snow, with a bracing air, and over fifteen degrees of frost. I have no occasion for a barometer, as I can tell by my moustache what the temperature is to a degree, according as it is limp, stiff, or stalactic. It was the latter to-day, as the frozen breath was hanging in long icicles down to the bottom of my chin; but how enjoyable the atmosphere, and how interesting the spot on which we are standing, for it was from here, that the advanced guard of the French army caught the first view of the golden Minarets and starry domes of Moscow, and the Kremlin burst upon their sight. "All this is yours," cried Napoleon, when he first gazed upon the goal of his ambition, and a shout of "Moscow! Moscow!" was taken up by the foremost rank and carried to the rear of his army. But the Russian army had marched out of the whole capital, with muffled drums, and colours furled, leaving the city to its fate, so that ere the night had closed in, and Napoleon arrived at the gate, he learnt to his astonishment and mortification that 300,000 inhabitants had fled, and that the only Russians who remained in the city were the convicts who had been liberated from the gaols, a few of the rabble, and the sick and wounded in the hospital, and it was soon discovered that the fire which had commenced could not be restrained, and fanned by the wind it spread rapidly, and consumed the best portion of the city. "The churches," says Labanne, "though covered with iron and lead, were destroyed, and with them those graceful steeples which we had seen the night before resplendent in the setting sun; the hospitals, too, which contained more than 20,000 wounded, soon began to burn—a harrowing and dreadful spectacle—and almost all these poor wretches perished!" Also, Karamzin writes, "Palaces and temples, monuments of art, and miracles of luxury, the remains of past ages and those which had been the creation of yesterday, the tombs of ancestors, and the nursery cradles of the present generation, were indiscriminately destroyed; nothing was left of Moscow save the remembrance of the city, and the deep resolution to avenge its fate. At length, on the 19th of October, after a stay of thirty-four days, Napoleon left Moscow with his army, consisting of 120,000 men and 550 pieces of cannon, a vast amount of plunder, and a countless number of camp followers. And now the picture of the advance was to be reversed, Murat was defeated at Malo-Yaroslavits on the 24th, and an unsuccessful stand was made at Viasma on the 3rd November. On the 6th, a winter, peculiarly early and severe, even for Russia, set in, the thermometer 18 degrees below freezing, the wind blowing furiously, and the soldiers struggling in vain with the eddying snow, could no longer distinguish the road, and falling into the ditches by the side, there found their grave. On the 5th of December, Napoleon left his army; on the 10th he reached Warsaw, and on the 18th Paris and the Tuileries." Thus ended the greatest military catastrophe that ever befel an army in either ancient or modern times. And who were the great Russian generals who counselled the destruction of their city, rather than the conqueror should possess it? De Tolly, and Kotusoff; and who was another great Russian general whose name has figured in history? Suwaroff. And we have stood at their graves in the churches of Kazan and Alexander Newski at St. Petersburg, and read these inscriptions:—

> Here lies Kotusoff.
> Here lies Suwaroff.

In the evening Louise and I walked alone for an hour on the terrace in front of this same Kremlin, with the full bright moon pouring its softened rays on this now peaceful city, and indulged in reflections on its past, its present, and as to what its future history might be; and so ended our visit to Moscow.

I remain, MY DEAR JOHN,

Your affectionate brother,

R. RICHARDSON-GARDNER.

HÔTEL DE RUSSIE,

ST. PETERSBURG,

22nd Jan.—(3rd Feb. 1872.)

MY DEAR JOHN,

Back again to our old quarters for a few days, and then off to Warsaw, on our homeward journey. We find a great difference between the climate of St. Petersburg and that of Moscow, the latter being much more healthy and bracing. For all that I would rather live at St. Petersburg, as it is always gay and lively. And now for a few words about the opera and theatres. Our first visit was to the Grand Opera House, where a Russian ballet, and nothing but ballet, went on for nearly four hours, the subject being the adventures of Don Quixote and Sancho Panza, the horse of the knight, and the ass of the squire, figuring prominently in the scenes. The dancing was most excellent, and I am pleased to say the *danseuses* bear irreproachable characters. No one is permitted to go behind the scenes, and they are all educated and taught at an academy provided by Government under professors of the terpsichorean art. There are among them a celebrated group of Polish dancers, who gave us in great perfection and in national costume, the Polish national dance, called the "Mazur." This must not be confounded, as it often is in England, with the "Mazurka." It is a totally different thing, as it is danced throughout by four couples with great *esprit* and *aplomb*. Another night we went to the Russian Opera House, where we were much entertained by an opera, the subject of which was the history of the first Romanoff, but who himself never appeared, it being forbidden that a representation of a member of the present reigning family should be placed upon the stage. The house was full of Russians of all ages and sizes, as, it being a popular and nationally historical opera, schools and children were brought to hear it. The opera houses and theatres in Russia are subsidised by the State, and are under the surveillance of a Government officer, who appoints directors to each establishment. The opera houses of St. Petersburg and Moscow are under the management of " Signor Eugéne Merelli, Regisseur en chef de l'Opera Imperial Italien de St. Petersburg et Moscow," to whom I had the pleasure of an introduction, and who very kindly sent us a box for a " Patti " night (not purchasable for money, as the boxes are either hereditary in families, or subscribed for the season), and who afterwards invited me to a soirée at his house, to meet all the artists and artistes of the grand opera, which I can assure you was a great treat. We had a most delightful evening, and among the guests were many whose names have been familiar to me as " household words " for years, and others, whose melodious notes have so often enchanted me at both the London opera houses. We had Arditi, *chef d'orchestre* and the following tenors :—Naudin; Bettini, husband of Trebelli-Bettini ; Corsi, son-in-law to Naudin ; and Nicolini, whose success has been greater at St. Petersburg than in London, as the music is sung here half a note lower, which suits his voice much better; also, Ciampi, the buffo ; Bagagiolo, the basso profundo ; and Madame Bagagiolo, a magnificent type of the true Italian woman ; Sinico, the pretty and piquante soprano ; and the handsome Trebelli, the celebrated contralto; and many others, all of whom were exceedingly polite and agreeable to your English brother, and what pleased him much was the enthusiasm with which they spoke of old England. Le Comte Brebinske, a non-professional guest like myself, gave " The health of Merelli," which was heartily responded to. Schneider is here at the Opera Bouffe, and we have had a Russian friend's box sent us twice, so we heard her in *La Grande Duchesse de Gerolstein* and in *Barbe Blue;* but I think her day is over. She is much too vulgar and in bad taste to suit any but Parisians.

Coming out of the opera we observed huge fires ascending from great cauldrons in the street, which had a very cheery effect, the object being that the servants in attendance with the carriages may get a warm up when the cold is intense. When the temperature is at ten degrees of frost the soldiers are furnished with a head-dress of Caucasian origin, called a *bashilick*. The ladies wear them also, made of fine materials from Circassia, and create rather a pleasing effect. Louise has invested in a couple, and was photographed in one last week. Talking of the cold, after twenty degrees of frost the Droshki drivers are not allowed to stand about in the street, as it has often occurred that after an extra drop of schnaps to keep the cold out they have fallen asleep in the night, and been frozen to death, the horses going home of their own accord to their stables with the Droshki and its unfortunate driver.

I took a Russian bath this morning, which was a novelty even to me, though I am an old Turkish bath bather. My bathman, who put me through the process, was a great strapping fellow, about three inches taller than myself. First of all, buckets of tepid water were thrown over me, and then followed a good lathering of soap, made up in a bowl, after which I was placed on a perforated board, through the holes of which hot steam began to percolate, which, getting hotter and hotter, and much too hot, although I can stand a good deal, I was obliged to sing out and make signs, when my bathman, mistaking my movements for a signal as to its not being hot enough, clapped on a little extra, which started me pretty quickly off my perforated bed, and I could not be induced to take another dose. I then observed six-foot-three provide himself with a cat-of-nine-tails, in the shape of a birch, made of bushes of the bay tree, and strongly suspecting when he got me at full length on my face he intended to administer this instrument, I respectfully requested to know (by signs, mind, as we could not speak a word to each other), what were his intentions, when he unhesitatingly informed me that it was part of the regular process, and must be proceeded with. I therefore resigned myself to my fate, went flat down on my face as directed, and got birched from my neck to my heels in true Spartan fashion, without wincing or moving a muscle; however, it was not as bad as I expected, as my tall friend took compassion on the tenderness of my skin, finding it not quite as tough as that of a Russian bear.

And now, my dear John, I must conclude this letter with one or two incidents which amused me while strolling out alone last Christmas-eve, when the Russians, like others, make more merry than usual. They are an extremely good-natured people, and seem to be still more so when in their cups, as most of the inebriated men seemed to have a tendency towards embracing everyone they met; I saw a good many peasants and working men   a partially obfuscated state during my walk, through some rather low thoroughfares, and was much entertained by finding that every man who was " half seas over " had always a sober companion to take charge of him. I afterwards discovered that this is a regular arrangement between two friends, Damon going in for enjoyment, while Pythias is held responsible for remaining sober, and the next outing they take the positions are reversed, Pythias giving way to the tempter, while Damon is bound to resist. I only found one exception during the night, when I saw two friends, who having for a long distance lunged against each other, at length lunged in the same direction, and over they went, rolling softly in the snow. Another fellow went head foremost into a snow heap, which had been piled up at the side of the road, and I assisted in dragging him out by his heels, where he would otherwise assuredly have been smothered. I saw another brought out of a Traktir by his sober friend, to the top of a staircase, and there he remained ever so long holding on by the rail, until his friend returned, but in the meantime I expected every minute to see him come rolling down the stairs; but no, he held on, and it became most difficult for his friend to get him away, which reminded me of a man on board the steamer from Kingston to Holyhead when we were crossing the Irish channel on one occasion. It was a stormy passage, and this poor fellow was awfully ill, and got hold of one of the foremost stays and stuck to it, although he was wet through and through, and the waves were continually breaking over him. None of the sailors could get him away, even by force, as it became rather dangerous, and they wanted to remove him; but he held on as though his life depended upon his retaining his hold of the stay. In my rambles, I at length heard a tremendous hallooing proceeding from a certain quarter, like the roar of a bull, but which I found to be the sonorous voice of a male Russian, who was undergoing being pinioned into a Droshki, his own son assisting in the operation. It seems, by what I could make out, by observation, that the son, a small boy, had followed his father during his tour of inebriation, no doubt by his mother's directions, until at length he called a policeman's attention to his parent, and had him brought out of the public, when the small boy duly produced from his pocket sundry straps, which he had providently brought with him for the purpose, and the sire being helpless, the dutiful boy, aided by the policeman, strapped him in the sleigh, and carried him home in triumph. While the father was hallooing like a mad bull, the small boy was grinning from ear to ear at his success, and evidently enjoying the fun.

Our stay here is now becoming short, we shall soon be " homeward bound," and so *adieu* until we meet.

I remain, MY DEAR JOHN,

Your affectionate brother,

R. RICHARDSON-GARDNER.

TO THE READER.

(Vide page 15.)

When these letters appeared last winter in the *Windsor and Eton Herald*, I received several communications from friends, questioning the correctness of my views with regard to the antagonistic feeling therein described to exist, between the Prussians and Russians, and the eventual probability of an alliance between the Russians and the French; but agreeing with me that the tone of feeling of foreign countries towards each other was naturally a matter of great importance to our own.

This morning, 18th December, 1872, I have read a most remarkable confirmation of some of my observations, in the letter of no less a person than the well-informed Prussian Correspondent of *The Times;* an extract from which I append:—

"*The Times,*" *Wednesday, December* 18, 1872.

GERMANY AND ITS NEIGHBOURS.

(FROM OUR PRUSSIAN CORRESPONDENT.)

BERLIN, DEC. 15.

This year's celebration of the Russian military festival of St. George has been again marked by the presence at St. Petersburg of some Prussian officers and the drinking of enthusiastic toasts in honour of the two armies and their "ancient *camaraderie.*" In strange contrast with these official demonstrations, the language of the Russian Press continues as hostile as ever to this country. When I say that three-fourths of the leading Russian papers are on principle opposed to their German neighbours, I am rather below the mark than otherwise. Hardly a day elapses without the Germans being in these organs either made the object of virulent attacks, or coolly charged with the design of acquiring influence and territory at Russia's expense. Distrust naturally begets distrust, and so we need not wonder that Russian politics should of late have been vigilantly scrutinized in this part of the world. In their estimate of Russia's position and strength, the German Press cannot of course overlook what has lately happened thousands of miles away on the distant banks of the Central Asian streams; and the remarks indulged in on this interesting topic are occasionally based upon the supposition that the ill-will so steadily shown this country by the Russian Press may some day influence the action of the Russian Government itself. The following reply to these German remarks is from the St. Petersburg *Mir* :—

"England regarding our position in Central Asia as more and more dangerous to herself, it is only natural that she should be seriously disquieted by the progress of our arms. But we confess we cannot conceive the motives of German journalists in constituting themselves the allies of the Anglo-Indians, and manifesting solicitude at the danger said to be threatening the dominion of the Calcutta Viceroy. This policy on the part of the German Press is the more startling from its being adopted just when the English journalistic agitation against us has somewhat cooled down. The only inference to be drawn from this is that the German Press is determined to oppose us, come what may, and to criticise our action, even in regions where Germany is utterly powerless to injure us. . . . . Some Berlin papers actually go the length of blaming the English for permitting us to deal with Khiva as we please. We do not know how far these attacks will be instrumental in heating the imagination of English politicians; but, whatever may be the result, there remains the interesting fact that German hostility to Russia has become so inveterate and irrepressible a feeling, that our Prussian friends have, in the midst of all their domestic troubles, time left to accord England the favour of their advice, though nobody has asked them for it."

It would be a work of supererogation to prove that the Germans can have no interest in entangling themselves with Russia, when they have so much else on their hands; nor is it at all necessary to demonstrate that the Russian Government having selected the principal object of its foreign policy in a southerly and easterly direction, is not particularly anxious to come to loggerheads with its formidable neighbour in the west. Yet so steady is the current of Russian public opinion in favour of France, and so noisily does it run in spiteful enmity against this people and Government, that, although the relations of the two Cabinets are as yet the very best, there is really no telling what may occur in the future.

www.ingramcontent.com/pod-product-compliance
Lightning Source LLC
Chambersburg PA
CBHW020256090426
42735CB00009B/1110